THE PROCESS OF PROPHECY

Truly awesome! This book is a prophetic voice that has embraced the loving nature of God and the season of grace that Jesus ushered in on the cross. The reader will clearly understand why prophetic judgment is not an option today and why God will not speak in a way that belittles or devalues a believer's life. Every word spoken in the name of God should be spoken in the hot pursuit of love and for lifting our head so we might gaze into the beauty of Father's tender loving eyes.

Jack Frost
Shiloh Place Ministries

Graham Cooke's new book, *The Process of Prophecy*, is destined to be one of the most practical tools the Holy Spirit will use to enrich and deepen the lives of many who desire to move more powerfully in the gift of prophecy. I love the way the book is structured and the very practical applications and readings at the end of the chapters. The sidebars telling the stories of great people in the kingdom of God who moved in prophecy after the apostolic age are a great encouragement to us who do believe God still speaks to His church. I am excited about this first of six books in this series that Graham will write. I will encourage its reading by the students at our Global School of Missions, Church Planting and Supernatural Ministry. I consider Graham Cooke one of the most respected persons I know who not only has a prophetic gift, but who is in the office of a prophet. It will be hard to find a more practical book to help you grow in prophecy. Graham has walked through many rough seasons in his life, and I am proud to watch him live out his life with great integrity and faithfulness to the author of all prophecy. Graham has been faithful to continue to bear the testimony of Jesus, which is the spirit of prophecy.

Randy Clark
Global Awakening

Once again, Graham Cooke delivers an extraordinary book on prophecy. His unique ability to communicate spiritual truth is refreshingly authentic and theologically sound. As one who ministers in the prophetic, I am indebted to the wisdom of years that Graham has put into this writing. *The Process of Prophecy* is truly a one-of-a-kind manuscript that reveals the heart and mind of one of the foremost prophets and thinkers in the church today. It is a must-read that will help you navigate through the deep waters of prophetic ministry.

Larry Randolph
Larry Randolph Ministries

I highly recommend Graham's new book. He has profound insights into the nature of the prophetic ministry and never loses sight of the practical application.

Jack Deere
Evangelical Foundation Ministries

Graham Cooke's writings and teachings always leave me hungering and thirsting for more — more of God, more divine revelation, more understanding of God's heart, ways and values. His writings whet my appetite for the deep things of the Spirit because the truths Graham presents come alive within my heart. *The Process of Prophecy* is full of divinely inspired revelatory treasures—treasures that took years of searching, refining and preparing to bring them as gifts to you, the reader. The richness of its contents reveals that the writer has truly paid a great price to pen its pages. I love this book!

Patricia King
Extreme Prophetic

In *The Process of Prophecy*, Graham Cooke has clearly articulated truth that is attainable and achievable. He demonstrates what is possible for those who are concerned to grow churches that announce and demonstrate the kingdom of God. Graham provides practical and incisive insight that releases a congregation to move forward together into who they are called to be. There is absolutely no doubt that this book will both initiate the way forward and build the future for churches that are intent on cultivating an appetite for God.

Peter McHugh
Senior Minister, C3Centre

I had hardly advanced into the first chapter when I ran smack into a classic Graham Cooke revelation. He wrote, "God is more interested in creating collaborative prophetic communities than He is in birthing a new generation of prophetic superstars." If this is so (and I think it is), then God will surely use the new book as a tool to shape the skills and disposition of a new generation of prophetic voices. This new generation will have the ability to collaborate with one another and the throne room in a manner that will build a canopy of agreement between heaven and Earth. Asaph taught his musician sons how to flow in the prophetic anointing of David's tabernacle, and I believe Graham's counsel will tune the instruments of the sons and daughters that God is raising to flow in the prophetic tabernacle that covers us in these last days.

Lance Wallnau
Lancelearning Group

I received a new level of faith in the prophetic reading this book. Graham reveals the intentionality of God's love and encouragement toward us, and makes it clear how we are to hear His voice, know His heart, and prophesy confidently.

Julie Anderson
Prayer for the Nations

There is a curious tendency in "Spirit-filled" church life to promote the giftings of the New Covenant Spirit in the context of what is really Old Covenant practice. No wonder that we struggle with certain anomalies. However, there is brilliant news! Graham Cooke's new book, *The Process of Prophecy*, is a significant and mature contribution to the prophetic teaching arena, and his approach is best summarized by his comment, "Any time someone receives a prophetic word, grace should explode in his heart." Well said! The rest of the book is consistent with that statement in both its well-developed content and it's easily implemented practical exercises. This book is worthy of wide endorsement and exposure. We need a healthy, life-giving approach to the understanding and practice of prophecy, and Graham manages to accomplish this extremely well.

David Crabtree
Senior Pastor, DaySpring Church, Sydney, Australia

I've always enjoyed Graham's writings and public ministry. His recent bite-size, interactive format is just in time for a faster thinking, activational, and demanding generation. He makes me think and take time to pause with insights that act as keys, unlocking my own creativity. Keep those keys coming—let's see what treasures lie ahead!

Steve Witt
Edify Ministries International
Author of *Experiencing Father's Embrace*

It's rare to find a prophet who can prophesy *and* train other to do the same! Graham's new book puts a rich treasure into the hands of the church, not just to understand the nature of the prophetic, but to develop a sensitive heart to the voice of God. When Graham first came to CFC 16 years ago, he prophesied many things which we are now walking in. But he also empowered us to develop the prophetic when he left. If you can't get Graham to come and visit you personally, then this book is a very close second! It imparts God's heart, has wonderful insights, is easily understood, and at the same time gives very practical instructions on how to develop the prophetic. I doubt if there is a better book on the prophetic in print.

Paul Reid
Leader, Life Link Team, Christian Fellowship Church, Belfast

In Graham Cooke's new book, *The Process of Prophecy*, he outdoes himself, as I've come to expect. He continually amazes me with each line in this book. How can one man come up with so many quotable quotes? Wow! Based solely on Scripture yet lived out in his own life, the content of Graham's new book will walk you through the real purpose for prophecy today. This book is about transition in the prophetic gift currently operating and accepted within the church. So, use this as a primer for yourself, your friends, or even your own church group. You will never think of prophecy in the same way again!

Steve Shultz
The Elijah List

My personal acquaintance with this author makes my endorsement to be both a privilege and a responsibility. There are few voices in the realm of the prophetic dimension in which there would be the freedom to recommend a book without reserve. Graham Cooke is one who has excelled in this needed realm. He has been given an unusual ability to remain biblically accurate and spiritually insightful while wrapping every instruction and expectation in the love of the Father. If your heart hungers to know and become involved in the prophetic dimension, don't hesitate to make this volume your very own.

Bob Mumford
Lifechangers

VOLUME TWO
2

THE PROCESS *of* PROPHECY

THE BEAUTIFUL STEPS OF MOVING IN PROPHECY

Graham Cooke

THE PROPHETIC EQUIPPING SERIES

The Process of Prophecy was formerly known as *Approaching the Heart of Prophecy*, Module Two.

Published by Brilliant Book House LLC
PO Box 871450
Vancouver, WA 98687

www.brilliantbookhouse.com

Copyright © 2020 by Graham Cooke

Requests for information should be addressed to:
E-mail: admin@brilliantperspectives.com

All rights reserved. No part of this book may be reproduced, stored in a retrieval system or transmitted in any form or by any means — electronic, mechanical, photocopy, recording, or otherwise — without prior written permission of the copyright owner, except by a reviewer who wishes to quote brief passages in connection with a review for inclusion in a magazine, newspaper or broadcast.

Unless otherwise indicated, all Scripture quotations are taken from The Holy Bible, New American Standard Version. Copyright © 1960, 1962, 1963, 1971, 1972, 1973, 1975, 1977, 1995 by The Lockman Foundation.

ISBN: 978-0-9896262-9-3

DEDICATION

To all my friends in the Prophetic Ministry who have learned to grow up in God in the midst of one of the most persecuted areas of ministry.

All comparisons are odious. All judgments are spurious, except the one at the end of the age.

Learning the ways of God opens our eyes to His truth and life which we portray and of which we speak.

The central themes of God's nature in the new man are the drivers of what we teach and how we prophesy.

The people I have enjoyed listening to, talking with, and being around in life have all left an imprint on my mind, heart, and spirit:

Graham Perrins, Gerald Coates, Martin Scott, Christine Noble, Jack Deere, Mike Bickle, James Goll, Kim Clement, Patricia King, John Paul Jackson, Larry Randolph, Kris Vallotton, Stacey Campbell, David Wagner, Paul Cain, Johnny Enlow, Brad Jersak, Christine Larkin, Shawn Bolz, Garry Morgan, Mark Iles, Jim Paul, Michael Sullivant, Scot Webster, Bill Hamon, Dena McClure, Dan McCollam, Peter Stott.

There is a larger list—these are my heroes. They have been tried, tested, and they have prevailed.

ACKNOWLEDGMENTS

If it takes a village to raise a child, then it takes an army of people to take territory and to keep it.

I know people who know how to fight for something. They stand in the presence of the ones who remain undefeated since the beginning.

The church needs a household of faith—a relational habitation that empowers trust, growth and maturity.

The kingdom requires an army—a disciplined body of people who are fixed on objectives and have the focus of warriors who know how to win.

If we are to take cities for God and raise up rural regions to encourage fullness in the face of warfare; then we must build churches that can prevail in the strategies and tactics of God.

We need the paradox of both household and army in order to accomplish our Kingdom role in the earth.

Lord, raise up the type of leaders that can break the grip of the world, the flesh, and the evil one.

ABOUT THE COVER

Much like life, design can be both a journey and an adventure with the Holy Spirit. While exploring visuals and options, His deep, soft presence is like the gentle pull of the compass—always sure, aligned, whispering a path to true north.

On this journey of life, I secure my confidence in the one thing that never changes—the steady company of our sure-footed Guide and Chief Encourager. The landscape of life's circumstances is guaranteed to change dramatically—unexpectedly morphing around us into deep depths of adversity. Or, just as quickly, these moments can open upon sweeping vistas of joyful breakthrough and revelation. During any trial or victory, God's steadfast hand is always present as He guides us onward and upward from within the beauty of His own heart—our authentic true north.

"Whether you turn to the right or to the left, your ears will hear a voice behind you, saying, 'This is the way; walk in it'" (Isaiah 30:21).

Dia Becchio, *Design*

TABLE OF CONTENTS

Introduction	xvii
The Process of Prophecy	5
Rejoicing Always	8
Meditation: Loving God with Your Mind	9
Waiting on God	17
The Heart Precedes the Mind at All Times	20
Soul and Spirit	32
Tongues	34
Unceasing Prayer	35
Prayer, Power, Process	41
Intimate Prayer	44
Pursue Love	47
New Beginnings	51
Three Phases of Revelation	56
Operating in Prophecy	62
Starting Where You Are	65
How Does Prophecy Come?	68
Being Quiet Is Key	86
Rhythm of Life with God	89
Give What You Have	90
Tongues and Interpretation	92
God Uses Everyday Objects	104

Reflections, Exercises, and Assignments	112
A Meditation and Reflection Exercise	152
What Kind of Partnership with Leaders?	155
What Help and Support from Leaders	156
A Prophecy	160
Recommended Reading	165
About the Prophetic Equipping Series	167
About the Author	169

INTRODUCTION

> *And it shall come to pass afterward that I will pour out My Spirit on all flesh; your sons and your daughters shall prophesy, your old men shall dream dreams, your young men shall see visions. And also on My menservants and My maidservants I will pour out My Spirit in those days.* (Joel 2:28–29)

THE WORLD CHANGED THE DAY the Holy Spirit fell on Jesus' remaining disciples in that famed upper room in Jerusalem. The Spirit of God, reserved in the Old Testament for a select few, had now been placed on anyone who sought and loved Christ. With that outpouring came the gifts of the Spirit. While once only a few could prophesy, suddenly everyone could.

I have been in the prophetic ministry since 1974. I began prophesying the year before. That's more than thirty years of sharing the love God has placed in my heart. Amazingly, I'm still learning—and I never want to stop. Every year, I understand something new about God and His ways. He never ceases to intrigue me.

More than a decade ago, my book *Developing Your Prophetic Gifting*, was first published. It has been a greater success than I could have ever imagined. It has gone through many reprintings; several publishers have taken it up; it has been written in many, many languages; and it still is on the best-seller list; and yet the material I teach now is light years beyond that original manuscript. I have come a long way in the years since I wrote that first book. For one thing, I have taught countless prophetic schools during that time. As I work with students and emerging prophetic voices, I have had my own gift shaped and honed.

"As iron sharpens iron, so a man sharpens the countenance of his friend," as it says in Proverbs 27:17. The people I have met have pushed me further into the things of the prophetic. They have challenged me to find fresh ways of equipping, explaining, and encouraging.

For several months, I have felt the Lord prompt me to rewrite *Developing Your Prophetic Gifting*, adding the material I have taught in my schools over the past ten years since it was published. This book is the first in a series of six that will more fully equip people longing to speak the words of God to those around them.

Following the unqualified success of the spirituality journals in the Being with God Series,[1] I have decided to develop this material into the same format.

Each book has assignments, exercises, and meditations that, if followed, will bring each individual into an experience of God within the context of the material.

Together, we will study the practical elements of hearing God, of moving in the Spirit, of knowing God's nature, and of representing His heart to someone else. We will learn how to be grounded in the love, grace, and rhythm of God. It is my prayer that these books will give you something fresh about who God wants to be for you. As you read the principles and illustrations within, I pray that you will be excited and inspired to venture further into what God has for you.

> **A SMALL MIND IS INCOMPATIBLE WITH A BIG HEART**

Prophecy comes when we have a burden to encourage and bless the people around us. There is no magic formula to prophesying; it all depends on our love for God. When we love Him fully, that love should

---

[1] See www.brilliantbookhouse.com for more information.

spill over onto the people around us. Prophecy is simply encouraging, exhorting, and comforting people by tuning them into what God has for them. In every church in the world, there are people who need that life-giving word from God. These aren't just the individuals who are obviously struggling; some appear to have everything together. But God knows what's really going on.

Everyone could benefit from a prophetic word, even those for whom everything is soaring. I love to prophesy over people who are doing really well. If we can target those people and increase their faith at a critical time, they can fly even higher in the things of the Spirit.

New Testament prophecy will be spoken through the context of the gospel of grace. Jesus has received the judgment of God for sin for all those who are living, to enable them to find repentance through the goodness and kindness of God.

Prophecy is now in the context of a family, a company of called-out people who are learning together to become the beloved of God, the Bride of Christ. There is a new language in the Spirit to learn and the unity of the Spirit to maintain and enjoy, as a people together.

Of course there are necessary tensions in all good relationships and prophecy is not the way to resolve conflicts. Clearly we need wisdom for those situations.

WHEN THE CHURCH RUNS OUT OF ENCOURAGEMENT, THE WORLD RUNS INTO WICKEDNESS

I believe strongly that the more encouraging, exhorting, and comforting prophecy we have, the better our churches will be. Blessing and encouragement stir up anointing. The more of this kind of prophecy we can have in church, the less we will need intensive, time-consuming pastoral care. People will actually be touched by God and come into the things of the Spirit themselves. Individuals will realize that, yes, they are loved personally by God. That kind of revelation will stoke their faith in ways a counseling session never could.

I know I need that kind of encouragement every day from the Holy Spirit. I can't remember the last time I asked Him to encourage me and He didn't. He may not speak it out immediately, but He always meets me at the point of my greatest need. That's just who the Holy Spirit is and what He loves to do.

This book can help you go further in the prophetic than you have ever hoped. After all, *"Eye has not seen, nor ear heard, nor have entered into the heart of man the things which God has prepared for those who love Him"* (1 Corinthians 2:9).

The Process of Prophecy is not a quick read. I encourage you to take your time going through this book, reading slowly and with your heart, until you understand the themes and thoughts they contain.

Furthermore, don't neglect the exercises, case studies, and Bible readings included at the end of each volume—they are valuable practice tools that will take the lessons taught and put them into practice in your life.

Throughout this book, I have included several sidebar articles about some of my prophetic heroes. These are people who lived after the Bible was finished being written, heard the voice of God for themselves, and did marvelous exploits for the Kingdom. I hope this will open your eyes to a few of the people who have gone before us.

I have also included some suggestions of resources that may help you further explore the themes contained in this book. I hope they prompt you to dig deeper into the things of the Spirit.

Blessings on your journey into the prophetic!

Graham

VOLUME TWO

THE PROCESS *of* PROPHECY

THE BEAUTIFUL STEPS OF MOVING IN PROPHECY

VOLUME TWO
The Process of Prophecy

WHAT YOU WILL LEARN IN THIS SEGMENT:

- How to come to God so that our prophesying is clean and pure.
- The power of meditation to reveal Presence.
- All joy belongs to the Father. It's who He is and therefore who we are too!
- The importance of stillness in waiting on God.
- Being renewed in the spirit of your mind.
- The spiritual life is powerfully possible when your soul comes under the rule of your spirit.
- Hearing and praying give huge impetus to knowing God's will.
- Process is the key to life in the Spirit. It is the process that makes us rich, not the outcome.
- Pursuing love as a prerequisite for moving in prophecy.
- Prophecy restores people's dignity and self-respect.
- Sensitivity to the Lord is the basis for all prophecy.
- The simple steps of moving in prophecy.
- Prophecy is released when we acknowledge a burden for an individual or a group of people.
- Living from your heart, not your head.

VOLUME TWO

The Process of Prophecy

WHAT YOU WILL LEARN IN THIS SEGMENT:

- How to receive revelation, not just information.

- The power of enlightenment in seeing from the heart.

- All knowledge leads to an actual experience of truth.

- Your perception is linked to your destiny.

- Your will is the vehicle for the spirit.

- Praying with God, not toward Him.

- Developing joyful routines that touch God's heart.

- The relationship between prayer, power and process.

- Pray like a bride, not a widow. Begging is not favor!

- To receive closure on the past and develop a present/future relationship with the Lord.

- There is always a new "you" emerging!

- The three phases of revelation.

- The simple power of expectation.

- Operating in the flow and ebb of life in the Spirit.

- How vision and dreams work and their purpose.

VOLUME TWO
The Process of Prophecy

WHAT YOU WILL LEARN IN THIS SEGMENT:

- Moving in what you see.

- Developing the relationship between prophecy and scripture.

- Hearing the whispers of God.

- Becoming attuned to the faint touches of God.

- Impression engages the heart of the person prophesying with the Holy Spirit.

- Everything comes from God and returns to God.

- Developing quietness is a key to being prophetic continuously.

- Developing the rhythm of your own fellowship with the Lord.

- Starting where you are and giving what you have.

VOLUME TWO

THE PROCESS *of* PROPHECY

IF PROPHECY, LIKE A WEBSITE, had a list of frequently asked questions, this one would top it: "When I'm moving in prophecy, how can I tell if it's me, the Lord, or the enemy?" I've been asked that question many hundreds of times over my thirty years in prophetic ministry.

It is a legitimate question. We are human beings, subject to pain, disillusionment, hurts, dreams, aspirations, longings, and desires. We sort, delete, distort, and repackage the mound of information we receive every day. Our humanity can conspire against us and color a prophetic word with a different hue than God intended. We can give into the power of "me."

We can also come under the influence of the enemy, either directly through bitter, unresolved issues in our lives, or indirectly through bad attitudes and a lack of good relationships. It is possible for a frustrated person to speak prophetically their own thoughts and opinions, mixing them with the words that God is really saying. The enemy can inspire that to happen and people could be moved by a spirit other than the Lord's, but this usually happens only when people have buried their hurts and rejection in real anger. Their lives become fertile ground for enemy activity. Alternatively, the enemy can use our unyielded thoughts and impulses, and as we speak out of our own soul, he can move in behind our words to cause mischief.

With these issues in mind, it is no wonder so many Christians fear polluting a prophetic word. How do we give a pure word of prophecy that glorifies the Lord, has no tinge from our hearts, and has no influence of the enemy attached? Further complicating this question is the issue of faith. Sometimes we may not be operating in complete certainty and we have to prophesy as far as our faith allows.

One thing can guarantee the purity of our prophecy—a large dose of humility. A humble spirit ensures that we will not seek to do anything to dishonor the Lord Jesus, discredit the ministry, or disrupt the body of Christ.

In this life, we either humble ourselves or we get humiliated. We either fall on the rock or it falls on us. Humility is not a natural characteristic in any of us. No one is born with it. Our relationship with God builds as we submit our lives, thoughts, and perspectives to Him. Our aim is to always live our lives in the best way possible, so that the Holy Spirit is made welcome in us. *"Create in me a clean heart, O God, and renew a steadfast spirit within me,"* as David sang in Psalm 51:10–11. *"Do not cast me away from Your presence, and do not take Your Holy Spirit from me."*

If we prophesy in humility and make a mistake, the Lord will give us grace to face the issue and put things right. Mistakes are inevitable as we learn how to move in the supernatural. That is why Paul was so clear in 1 Thessalonians 5:19–21 — *"Do not quench the Spirit. Do not despise prophecies. Test all things; hold fast what is good."* We need to be able to sift and separate the good from the bad, the misguided, and the misinterpreted.

AIMEE SEMPLE McPHERSON

Lived: 1891 to 1944

Prophetic Synopsis: Born in rural Canada, Aimee accepted Christ at age seventeen in a revival meeting led by Robert Semple. Months later, she married Semple and traveled with him to China to spread the gospel there. Upon their arrival in Hong Kong, however, both contracted malaria. Aimee was a few months pregnant when Robert died.

Alone, terrified, sick, pregnant, and just nineteen, Aimee called out to God. "Morning after morning of the month that followed, I would wake up with a scream as my great loss swept over me," she said. "Then the Comforter would instantly spring up within me until I was filled with joy unspeakable, and my hot, dry eyes would flow with tears of love and blessing." **Aimee eventually gave birth to a little girl, worked hard, and made enough money for the two to return to America.**

After remarrying, God called Aimee to preach. For months, she wrestled with that call. She had another child and eventually had a nervous breakdown.

As she laid in her bed, not sure if she was going to live or die, Jesus appeared to her and said, "Go preach My Word." Aimee made excuses as to why she couldn't, but Jesus was adamant: "Do the work of an evangelist. The time is short; I am coming soon." **The moment she accepted the call, God healed her.**

Eventually, Aimee moved to Los Angeles and planted a church. She arrived in 1921 with just a tambourine and ten dollars, and opened a 5,300-seat church—debt-free—a year later. The walls of her church were lined with the crutches, wheelchairs, and canes of the people God healed. Her illustrated sermons were copied by Hollywood: she rode in on a motorcycle once, and hired dozens of animals on another occasion. During the Great Depression, she set up a food bank and free store, helping 1.5 million people.

Key Comment: "All I could do was say one word when I prayed: Jesus!"

Sources: Stanley Burgess and Gary McGee, editors, *Dictionary of Pentecostal and Charismatic Movements* (Grand Rapids, MI: Zondervan (9th printing), 1996). Roberts Liardon, *God's Generals* (Tulsa, OK: Albury Publishing, 1996).

With the help of the Holy Spirit, we must ensure that we live our lives in the best way possible. There must be no part of us that does not belong to Jesus. Our lifestyle must be full of rejoicing, meditation, prayer, healing, waiting on God, love, and expectation.

REJOICING ALWAYS

Rejoicing is a key ingredient in moving in the power and presence of God. Many Christians have been conditioned to think that they enter God's presence with prayer. But Scripture is clear that thankfulness is the door to His presence—*"Enter into His gates with thanksgiving, and into His courts with praise. Be thankful to Him, and bless His name,"* says Psalm 100:4.

It is not a coincidence that rejoicing precedes prayer without ceasing. Our stillness is dependent on our gratitude. Whatever happens, we must thank God for the set of circumstances we are in. I'm not saying that we must thank God for something horrible that has happened: Christians are not called to be masochists. However, we can thank God that He is always with us.

AN ALWAYS REJOICING HEART IS THE KEY TO LISTENING TO GOD

Rejoicing in God gives us the opportunity to hear Him. When we enter His presence with thanksgiving, we open more of ourselves to His voice. *"In everything give thanks; for this is the will of God in Christ Jesus for you,"* Paul wrote in 1 Thessalonians 5:18. When we want to know God's will for a situation, we begin by giving thanks.

Probably two-thirds of the rest of the world would change places with us in the West in a heartbeat, no matter how poor our lifestyle. To many, we are rich beyond their wildest dreams. Count your blessings;

there are so many things to give thanks for. If we struggle with being grateful to God for what He has given us, chances are we will be ungracious to people in how we live our lives. It is disciplines like gratitude, thanksgiving, praise, and worship that keep the presence of God fresh and alive in our hearts.

This is a fundamental spiritual truth that can reshape and reignite our personal time with God. By entering His presence with praise, not petitions, we learn how to adore God. Our hearts become full of constant, continuous worship. We are people called to be happy in God; if we don't have joy in our relationship with Him, how can we expect anyone else to?

As a Christian, who would you rather be represented by: the most miserable individual on Earth, or the happiest person in the world? This is the very choice God faces! Nobody wants to be represented by someone who is glum and miserable. Adoration helps us remain happy in God.

MEDITATION: LOVING GOD WITH YOUR MIND

I love having quiet times with God. There is nothing like experiencing God's love, touch, and blessing in stillness with Him. His job is to be our Lover; ours is to be His beloved. I love letting God touch me. He draws me into Him, erasing all of the striving, pressure, frustration, and frantic pace of life.

Meditation is about finding our rhythm with God. When we couldn't have cared less about Him, God couldn't have cared more. Before we knew Him, He took the initiative and reached out to us. *"We love Him because He first loved us,"* says 1 John 4:19. We responded to what He did, and He answered our response. Like a dance, we went back and forth—and we still do. God moves; we move. The Father works; we work. The Holy Spirit engages; we engage. Everything we do flows out of our relationship with God. Meditation provides us with the inward anointing to reveal the Presence of God.

All of life in the Spirit flows from the inside out—coming from the inner man of the Spirit, through the soul as a vehicle of expression that uses our body to demonstrate to the outside world who we really are in the Spirit.

Meditation is a fabulous spiritual discipline that enables us to see in the Spirit. It is the eyes of our heart being enlightened so that we can know (i.e., understand and experience) who God is for us (see Ephesians 1:18).

Prayer is the process of finding out what God wants to do and then asking Him to do it. Meditation is an important precursor to that effort. Before we pray, we ought to meditate, read, think, listen, and be still. Reading the Bible does reveal the will of God to us because confidence and prayer go together. By meditating on the Word of God, the way I pray is shaped.

Several months ago, our church leadership team read Romans 8:35–39 together:

SPIRIT LIFE FLOWS FROM THE INSIDE OUT

> *Who shall separate us from the love of Christ? Will tribulation, or distress, or persecution, or famine, or nakedness, or peril, or sword? Just as it is written:*
>
> *"For Your sake we are being put to death all day long; We were considered as sheep to be slaughtered."*

But in all these things we overwhelmingly conquer through Him who loved us. For I am convinced that neither death, nor life, nor angels, nor principalities, nor things present, nor things to come, nor powers, nor height, nor depth, nor any other created thing, will be able to separate us from the love of God, which is in Christ Jesus our Lord.

The difficulty is that our emotions can become bigger than the gospel if we let them.

Emotions can be as strong and as hard to arrest as a runaway horse. We can place more power and emphasis on them than the revealed word of God in scripture.

"I feel really disconnected from God," we say. However, we fail to see that against what the Lord says in scripture: "I will never leave you nor forsake you." "I am with you always." "Nothing can separate you from My love!"

Reading a passage like the above can infuse Christians with confidence. What a great thing to pray! Nothing can separate us from the love of God: by meditating on it, this truth embeds itself deep within our spirits. Our minds become renewed through the power of God's love. We give our inner being the opportunity to access the Holy Spirit and be changed.

In Psalm 46:10, God gave us an important instruction: *"Be still, and know that I am God."* Stillness releases a capacity in us to receive truth at a deeper level. *"Now may the God of peace Himself sanctify you completely; and may your whole spirit, soul, and body be preserved blameless at the coming of our Lord Jesus Christ,"* Paul wrote in 1 Thessalonians 5:23–24. *"He who calls you is faithful, who also will do it."* Learning how to cooperate with the Holy Spirit in the midst of problems and difficulties is vital. Without that help, we miss the wealth of our spiritual journey.

It is perfectly possible to bring ourselves to a place of peace. It is a simple discipline. Having practiced this for thirty years, I can now bring myself to peace in any situation within ten seconds. I have learned how to retreat back into my spirit and find the peace of stillness that meditation births in me. It has become simple for me, like using a computer or driving a car. Without stillness, our experience of God is limited. Stillness is a precursor to rest in the Lord, drawing us into a continual experience of His presence.

Put simply, we have to hear God's silence before we can listen to His voice. A silence exists in God that is so knowing, so healing, so releasing, and so embracing, that all kinds of things can be communicated to your heart. The silence is almost deafening: *"Deep calls unto deep at the noise of Your waterfalls; all Your waves and billows have gone over me,"* as the psalmist sang (Psalm 42:7). That capacity to enter stillness can release an unbroken communion with God and bring us into a place of being God-conscious.

The Lord does not cause the difficulties in our lives but He does know how to take advantage of opportunities!

God uses problems and issues to teach us how to be still. God uses every issue in several different ways because He is constantly at work in our lives. All too often we pray, "Lord, set me free from this," when He wants to work on five or six attitudes, conditions, and character issues in our life. "I'll set you free eventually," God says, "but I'd like to cover half a dozen of these things first. If you cooperate with Me, the benefits of this problem are going to be significant."

In the Spirit, every problem comes complete with its own provision attached. God is so kind that He will not let you experience an issue without His provision coming with it. Every problem is designed to bring us into something new in our experience of God. He allows in His wisdom what He could easily prevent by His power.

Meditation helps us discover that provision by reminding us of how reliant we are on God. In recent times, meditation has become a dirty word in some Christian circles because of its connection to the New Age and Eastern religions. However, meditation has been a part of humanity's relationship with God for thousands of years. The psalms, for example, are a series of meditations and are full of humans expressing their need to meditate.

When we consider deeply the things of God, we are meditating. When we reflect on His work in our lives, we have begun to meditate. It doesn't hurt to sit down and think about Jesus and meditate on the type of person He is. For me, I am constantly drawn back to how kind God has been to me. He is the kindest, happiest, and sunniest person I have ever met. I believe that when we get in contact with heaven, we will hear laughter. When we really come into the presence of God, tremendous joy, well-being, and peace flood our lives.

Joy is who God is, where He lives from, and what He does. He lives in perpetual, everlasting and eternal joy. In His presence there is fullness of joy. The Father does not give us joy. He gives us Himself. He is absolute joy personified. The atmosphere surrounding God is always joyful. We need to anchor our souls in the person of God and embrace His uninhibited delight in all things.

EVERY PROBLEM COMES WITH IT'S OWN PROVISION ATTACHED.

When we rejoice it is because we have entered the place of His joy and delight. We center ourselves in His joy. We breathe it in. We smile because we live under His smile. We rejoice because He is delight and delightful.

Whenever we encounter the Kingdom we are lovingly confronted with the God who loves to celebrate! We come under the influence of His innate joyfulness. When life is tough then we have permission to count it all joy (James 1:2-3)!

Joy is meant to overwhelm every negative emotion. "Sorrow and sighing may last for a night but joy comes in the morning" (Psalm 30:5). When joy is present no negative emotion can flourish. Jesus was acquainted with grief (see Isaiah 53:3); it was a close traveling companion. We need to be restored to the joy of our salvation, the delight and pleasure of our first major contact with the Lord. Joy keeps all experience in God fresh. New every morning are God's goodness and compassion (see Lamentations 3:21–23). Life in the Spirit is daily renewable and joy is always a part of God's day for us. It is His plan for us to be joyful on a constant basis. "These things I have spoken to you, that your joy may be full" (John 15:11).

Several years ago at a church weekend, I became aware of a man who had been going through an awful, miserable time. In a meeting, I felt compelled to lay my hands on him and pray for him to be refilled with the Holy Spirit. He fell on the floor and laughed for about half an hour. He really laughed; we couldn't do anything. The meeting went haywire, as God's joy took hold of him and the rest of the room, and we laughed and laughed and laughed. Through his joy, God began to fill the rest of us.

In recent years, I have seen some disturbing counterfeits of this, with some people charging big fees to bring the joy of the Lord into churches. I believe strongly that the joy of the Lord cannot be called up like some genie out of a bottle. It is not a spiritual manifestation that comes at the request of man. It is the by-product of the indwelling presence of God as He sovereignly and graciously causes rivers of living water to rise up within our hearts. The joy of the Lord comes from within.

> **THE FATHER SURROUNDS HIMSELF WITH JOY.**

Meditation can be a long process. Sometimes, I have spent several weeks on one particular passage of Scripture. When God is speaking to me clearly about something, there is not much point in reading something else. This is the underlying principle behind the *Lectio Divina* exercises we have included in this manual: we have to become disciplined in exploring the truth God is entrusting us with.

It is amazing how God uses meditation to share His heart with us. Years ago, the Lord spoke to me about working in the Caribbean. My flesh was fully saying "Yes and Amen" to that idea! Following that revelation, I enjoyed a private, ongoing joke with God about my "island ministry in the sun." Even as I spent years in the rain and the draughty cold of backstreet British churches, I chuckled with God: "One of these days, Lord, You will give me my desert island ministry." For several months, God spoke to me about the Caribbean. Other people would give me prophetic words about it. It seemed like just a matter of time.

One day, while speaking at a prophetic conference in London, I met a man quite by chance. I had just completed a seminar and was sitting quietly during a coffee break in the office of the senior pastor. The pastor had left me and another visitor alone together. At the time,

I was exhausted and only really thinking about coffee and rest. The man and I struck up a conversation about the conference I was leading. I gave him a brochure, thinking he was a local man who might wish to attend the event over the next few days.

Instead, the man said he wanted to stage a similar conference at his home church. It was at that point that I discovered that Dr. Noel Woodroffe led a church in Trinidad. He asked me if I would come and speak at his event. To be honest, I thought he was just being polite. However, a few months later, Noel sent me a plane ticket and my long-standing joke with the Lord was over. Noel was only at that London church for a few moments, but it was long enough for the two of us to meet and forge a friendship.

All of us have experienced situations where completely unforeseen things have happened and altered the course of our lives in different areas. It's good to sit down once in a while and think back on what God has done for us in the past several years. It's good to meditate on our own life and God's role in it. God Himself does this in heaven, according to Malachi 3:16:

> *Then those who feared the LORD spoke to one another, and the LORD listened and heard them; so a book of remembrance was written before Him for those who fear the LORD and who meditate on His name.*

WAITING ON GOD

Meditation is all about waiting on God and giving ourselves the time and space to be in communion with Him. This is not an unfocused event, but carries a deep sense of purpose: we want to be open to hearing God's voice everywhere. I constantly carry a notebook with me because God speaks to me in the most peculiar places. I haven't found a shower-proof notebook yet, but I'll buy one the day they are invented!

Sometimes waiting on God means letting God know that you actually love Him, that He's important to you, and that you take pleasure in who He is. There are times when we will wait on Him and nothing will happen. That's okay, for if God does not speak initially, He will always speak eventually. We need to be ready when He does.

Waiting on God is born out of a spirit of quiet and stillness. We have to calm the clamoring thoughts within our minds and hearts. Meditation and waiting on God go hand in hand; one often births the other. It fills our minds with thoughts of God and we become God-conscious. Into the quiet, God drops His words like the morning dew, refreshing our souls and spirits.

Conquering this discipline in private will deepen your public ministry. I once asked a professional tennis player how he dealt with one-hundred-mile-per-hour serves coming at him.

"You come to a place in your reactions where you're expectant of the ball coming across the net," he told me. "You have to develop an inner quietness, a watchfulness, and slow down your heartbeat so that the tennis ball looks like a football coming at ten miles per hour. You need that kind of mental capacity. Your

REST IS A WEAPON!

reaction, physical ability, and knowledge of how your opponent plays all combine together and you see things ahead of time."

The player was not a Christian, but his explanation translates perfectly into the world of the prophetic. Being in the presence of God slows down our heartbeat. It slows down our reactions and calms us on the inside. The louder it is on the outside, the quieter we must become on the inside.

My ability to quiet myself before God has allowed me to hear His voice in the most pressure-packed circumstances. Many years ago, I was in a Pentecostal church. There was a time of worship that was absolutely excruciating to be a part of. I was squirming in my seat and apologizing to God because I couldn't join in. I knew the songs — I just didn't think they should be sung that way.

"Lord, I'm really struggling with this worship," I prayed. "I'm sorry. To be honest, we've had fifty minutes of mindless singing and I'm really quite bored."

"It's alright for you; you're only visiting this place," I heard God whisper back to me. "I have to be here every week."

The pastor concluded the singing with a time of "waiting on the Lord." After a few moments, an elegantly dressed woman stood up, came to the microphone, and said the Lord had given her a vision.

"I see a penguin, halfway up a flagpole, with a carrot in its ear," she said. I wish I could make something like that up, but it is literally what she said. I sat still on the platform and waited, with everyone else, for an interpretation. Suddenly, I realized that everyone was staring at me and expecting me to interpret this mess!

I sat there with a mental picture of a penguin, carrot in ear, clamoring up a flagpole. It made no sense, and God wasn't showing or telling me anything about it. The main leader walked across the stage and knelt beside me.

"What's the Lord showing you?" he whispered.

"Nothing," I replied.

"Well, what do you think of the vision?" he tried again.

"I think you should tell her to stop eating cheese before coming to church — it's nonsense," I answered. "I mean, carrots and penguins and flagpoles? It's nonsense."

The pastor got indignant. "She's our most spiritual sister!" he said. "You need to go and give the interpretation."

"But there isn't one," I protested.

"There must be one," he said. "She's given the vision."

"I think you ought to discipline her," I replied. It was as though we were speaking two different languages. In the end, I had to go to the front and tell everyone that there was nothing supernatural about the vision. The whole place was silent as she jumped up and stormed out of the room. A whole group of people followed her, including the pastor. When things had settled down, I did some teaching.

After the meeting, I was called into the pastor's study and disciplined. It turned out that she was the biggest giver in the church and could do anything she liked, even give an oddball prophecy. The church lived in unreality.

Unreality occurs where Christians are not operating out of rest and peace, but live according to the whims of the external pressures they face. It sparks a form of mental gymnastics where revelation cannot penetrate. The mind is the enemy of the spirit — and the spirit is where God deposits His revelation. It takes faith for our conscious mind to accept the things our spirit tells us.

THE HEART PRECEDES THE MIND AT ALL TIMES

Sometimes, God asks us to do something unreasonable, and our minds try to talk us out of it. The mind deals with information, and the spirit with revelation. It can be difficult for those two elements to coexist. But we must submit our mind to our spirit, as counseled in 1 Corinthians 2:14— *"But the natural man does not receive the things of the Spirit of God, for they are foolishness to him; nor can he know them, because they are spiritually discerned."* We can only discern a prophetic word in our spirit.

We must return to the roots of our inherent spirituality and begin to believe as the early Christians did, who practiced their walk with the Lord.

When we became Christians we did not invite Jesus into our head: Faith is primarily an affair of the heart, not the mind. Our mind will undoubtedly play its part but not from a place of logic but spiritual intuition because we must all daily "be renewed in the spirit of our mind" (Ephesians 4:23).

We received salvation from a fragment of the truth. We did not know the whole bible nor the whole history of Jesus. Someone and something touched our heart and we opened up to the claims of the Kingdom.

Our heart needs less data than our mind. Our spirit receives revelation; our mind can only process information. When Jesus walked on water, half His disciples were terrified thinking it was a ghost. Peter said "If it's you, Lord, bid me come." Jesus did not throw Peter an instruction manual on how to walk on water. He just smiled enigmatically and said one word. "Come" was all He said, and on the strength of that one word Peter walked on a substance he had no business being on, except that he had permission.

The mind acting alone will always require more information. It will have more questions and will want everything dotted and crossed before it makes a decision. The problem with that is that God will not explain Himself. He does not make proposals for our approval.

The heart is designed to respond to revelation; the mind is not. When we are renewed in the spirit of our mind, it is because it has come under the rule of the heart regarding revelation.

The heart responds to God's Word in revelatory form. The mind follows the heart, and our mind is empowered to think through the how-to of God's instruction. The command instruction to obey comes from the heart.

The way that we come into salvation is the way that salvation is sustained. As Jesus is established in our heart by the Holy Spirit, we are also taught how to think as He thinks. Our mind must be under the rule of our heart or we are rendered useless for believing the impossible. The mind by itself can only rise to a possibility of something miraculous. We give mental assent to something without acknowledging the reality of it in spiritual terms.

It is our heart that recognizes the voice of God and sees His imprint on a situation. Our heart rises to the probability that something amazing is about to occur. We believe.

ONLY THE HEART CAN RECEIVE REVELATION

Repentance is not just about thinking again; it is about turning our thinking away from mere logic to having the mind of Christ. True repentance is a wonderful invitation to think as Jesus would think about the issue or situation in front of us.

If our spirit does not win the battle for primacy with the soul, then our faith will always be at the mercy of our logic. A logical, analytical mind will always talk us out of a supernatural experience. It is not difficult to tell who is a soulish Christian for they always need reassurance. Their head is in charge of their spirituality, so faith always gives way to logic and reason. The possibility of the Holy Spirit coming into our lives with His wonderful cheerfulness and abounding confidence is always much reduced when intellectualism rules our faith.

Of course I realize that we need great thinkers and key intellects in the Kingdom, but never at the expense of faith, childlike trust, and the creative imagination so vital to a life being led by the Spirit.

Our hearts must increasingly come to a new place of enlightenment where we can see in the Spirit.

> *In Him, you also, after listening to the message of truth, the gospel of your salvation—having also believed, you were sealed in Him with the Holy Spirit of promise, who is given as a pledge of our inheritance, with a view to the redemption of God's own possession, to the praise of His glory. For this reason I too, having heard of the faith in the Lord Jesus which exists among you and your love for all the saints, do not cease giving thanks for you, while making mention of you in my prayers; that the God of our Lord Jesus Christ, the Father of glory, may give to you a spirit of wisdom and of revelation in the knowledge of Him.*

> *I pray that the eyes of your heart may be enlightened, so that you will know what is the hope of His calling, what are the riches of the glory of His inheritance in the saints, and what is the surpassing*

greatness of His power toward us who believe. These are in accordance with the working of the strength of His might which He brought about in Christ, when He raised Him from the dead and seated Him at His right hand in the heavenly places, far above all rule and authority and power and dominion, and every name that is named, not only in this age but also in the one to come. And He put all things in subjection under His feet, and gave Him as head over all things to the church, which is His body, the fullness of Him who fills all in all. (Ephesians 1:13–23)

The Holy Spirit comes to each believer to enable them to realize, receive, and inherit every promise that the Father has set aside for them. Our faith grows exponentially as those promises become a reality and we learn progressively to live in the favor of God in the face of Jesus Christ.

In that context for life, it is so vital that "the eyes of our heart are enlightened." It is part of our inheritance in Christ that we perceive all of life from the Father's perspective. Knowing what the Lord thinks about any issue is a normal and necessary part of our relationship with Him.

THE MIND RECEIVES INFORMATION

The role of the Holy Spirit is to make us aware of how the Lord is thinking and also to release to us in visual form the insights and intentions of the Father. We have eyes to see and ears to hear all that the Father would impart to us. This is such a tremendous, close, and intimate relationship that we have with Jesus. There is no value in ignorance when our destiny is confidence. "*They that know their God shall be strong and do exploits*" (Daniel 11:32).

We are learning to live from our inner witness of the Holy Spirit and His presence in our lives. He is fully aware of heavens plans and lives to make us just as conscious and familiar with the Father's intention. The Holy Spirit is a brilliant teacher who seeks to develop our understanding and practice of seeing from the heart and living in a place of sensitivity. On every level He instructs us in righteousness, which is right living across all the spectrum of life, particularly in the matter of faith and obedience.

There is no substitute for sensitivity and obedience as the driving force of childlike trust and mature faith. We are compelled to become sensitive, finely tuned, susceptible and responsive to the Father's nature. Our heart will develop an acute sense of perception that is delicate and powerful. This is an awareness not rooted in mere head knowledge but is an actual spiritual, emotional, physical, and mental experience of God. The Father overwhelms all our senses and faculties in His pursuit of fullness in our lives. Fullness is concerned with touching every part of our being and releasing us to have great awareness of the love and joy of the Lord.

GOD SPEAKS THROUGH OUR HEART TO OUR MIND

The Holy Spirit will give us "a spirit of wisdom and revelation" so that our knowledge of God does not get stuck at the mental level. Knowledge in this context is always tied into an experience of God rather than just an intellectual notion of Him. Knowledge that does not lead to a deeper relational and spiritual experience of God is not worth the knowing. Our mind is touched but our heart is unchanged.

We are enlightened so that "we will know" what the mind of the Lord is and how to experience His thinking over us. The first commandment is to "*love the Lord your God with all your heart, and with all your soul, and with all your mind*" (Matthew 22:37).

This involves loving the Lord with everything that we are and have within ourselves. Our mind comes last in the order of loving simply because it can never be first. The mind can only follow the heart; it must never lead. When the mind leads we are reduced in our capacity to experience. It is our heart that has opened up to Jesus. It is our heart that has received His life and presence. It is our heart that is the doorway to an ongoing experience of His life.

WHEN OUR HEART PERCEIVES, OUR MIND CAN KNOW

We now live from the inside out. Our soul comes under the rule of our inner man. Our will and our emotions are governed by intimacy and sensitivity to the nature of God. In that context our mind is set free to love the Lord and to enjoy His thoughts.

Wisdom and revelation enter our spirit and our thinking, and our mindset is renewed and enables us to live at a higher level of thought and perception. Wisdom is superior to knowledge. Wisdom is a Christian context in the understanding of how the Father sees, how He thinks, and how He likes to do things. It is through wisdom that we develop a knowledge of God and His ways. Knowledge emanating from wisdom is the perception of thought leading to an experience of God's nature and a way of behaving that is consistent with confidence that produces faith.

To love God with your mind is to be drawn into an invited experience of knowing His thoughts. I love the way God thinks! When we allow ourselves to think as He does, our minds cease to be a battleground and instead become a place where we love the Lord and His thinking. Meditation, the act of deep thought, becomes a place of worship and intimacy with the mind of Christ. We are designed to practice intimate thinking with the Lord Jesus.

All our thoughts therefore lead us to joy and the presence of God. Our mind, following our heart, is now enabled and empowered to support the heart with love and intimate thinking. Thus are we consistently renewed in the spirit of our mind so that we are consumed by Christ's mindset.

TRUTH ONLY SETS US FREE WHEN IT BECOMES AN EXPERIENCE!

This is true enlightenment! It can only occur as the eyes of our heart are opened and made aware of the greatness of God. We are never overwhelmed by life when we are undone by the majesty of God's lovingkindness. Enlightenment makes us luminous in the glory of God's nature. We see the light about everything and our hearts are made light. We walk in the light of His thinking, intentionality, and loving intimacy. He lifts up the light of His countenance upon us (see Psalm 4:6). What a poetic and beautiful description of smiling!

He causes His face to shine upon us (see Psalm 80:3, 7, 19). His very graciousness is a wonderful tonic leading to total peace and blessing (see Deuteronomy 6:22–27).

From the place of wisdom and revelation our heart is enlightened and enlarged to live in a place of simplicity, sensitivity and trust so that we will know who God is for us at any moment.

Meditation is not just a place of deep thought. It is also a place of deep worship and intimate contemplation of the nature of god. Out from that place of internal rest and stillness we hear the word of the Lord and our thinking is corrected.

This is one of the laws of life in the Spirit, when God speaks from His heart we can never respond in our head. He is not looking for mental assent but a heart response. He does not seek our logical agreement or permission. We must respond in the medium of the message: heart to heart.

The Father always communes twice over an issue, speaking directly and indirectly. When our heart has received, responded, and obeyed His word, then our mind is flooded with revelation releasing strategies and tactics of how to move forward in our obedience. Faith grows by hearing and hearing by the word of God (see Romans 10:17). Our trust and sensitivity to the Holy Spirit promote obedience, which creates movement and momentum. Faith is active. Our mind needs to become responsive.

This is precisely what being led by the Spirit means! Our mind serves our heart. Knowledge serves faith and our will is serving our obedience, causing us to have greater experiences of God in the context of our current circumstances.

This is a critical discipline for us to recover at this time, otherwise what the Father speaks to us will make no sense. A heart response opens the mind to receive all the possibilities. If we respond to God's heart only with our head, then logic and reason will close the door to the supernatural. We will be reduced to only having options in the natural world because the possibilities of heaven will be shut out.

YOUR MIND MUST SERVE YOUR HEART OR YOU CANNOT FULLY KNOW GOD

When the eyes of our heart are enlightened, our sensitivity to the Holy Spirit enables our creative imagination to begin to see what God is saying. This is so vital if we are to believe all that the Lord has in store for us. Our assignment in the Kingdom is in direct proportion to our identity in the eyes of the Father.

Moses had to lead over a million people from bondage to a tyrant into freedom, and then into full release as a nation in their own territory. In order for this to occur he had to see himself in a particular way. The Lord needed Moses to step up into a higher place of awareness so that his heart could operate at a higher dimension of faith and power.

In that context the Lord speaks these remarkable words to him in Exodus 7:1:

> *Then the LORD said to Moses, "See, I make you as God to Pharaoh, and your brother Aaron shall be your prophet."*

If you do not see it, you cannot become it. Identity must be visualized before it can be realized. If Moses does not see this high place of living, then he will be forced to speak to Pharaoh from a lower state of being. He will be reduced to asking for favors, just like all the rest of the people at Pharaoh's court. Faith is then diluted to supplication instead of command. It is vital that Moses speaks to Pharaoh from this heightened sense of who he is in the Lord. Moses has to come at Pharaoh from a higher level of identity than Pharaoh himself possesses. Anything less and the assignment is not possible. "See! I have made you as God to Pharaoh." In other words, by the time that the Father has finished with Pharaoh, he will only be able to view Moses in his limited understanding of things. That is, Moses must be some sort of God in human form. Ironically, this is the spiritual perception that Pharaoh has been taught to have of himself. This means then that the king of Egypt is about to meet more than his match at this level!

IF YOU DON'T SEE IT, YOU CANNOT BECOME IT!

Pharaoh has massive authority and will only respond to someone who demonstrates more.

We see the same truth about visual perception in Joshua 6:1-2:

Now Jericho was tightly shut because of the sons of Israel; no one went out and no one came in. The LORD said to Joshua, "See, I have given Jericho into your hand, with its king and the valiant warriors."

See! See in your heart that I have given you Jericho, its king, and the best of his battle-hardened warriors. The heart response is to "see" what the Lord is proclaiming over you and to return that image to the Lord in confession and declaration. "Lord, thank You that You have made me this person already in the Spirit. I confess that my life and current experiences are therefore all geared to cooperating with the Holy Spirit to enable what You see to become my absolute present reality. Therefore I declare that my will is given over to You that the person You see in me shall emerge in this day for such a time as this." Or as Mary put it succinctly, "behold the bondservant of the Lord, be it done to me according to your word" (Luke 1:38).

Everything in Christ Jesus is Yes and Amen! God's heart says yes! In matters of the heart between you and the Father, reason must take its cue from divinely inspired imagination moving in trust and faith. The only time God will speak to your reasoning is when you have sinned. Then He says, *"Come now let us reason together, though your sins be as scarlet, yet they shall be as white as snow"* (Isaiah 1:18). Even here He invites us to "see" by using pictorial language. Mostly the Father invites our hearts into an experience of trust.

> *Trust in the LORD with all your heart and do not lean on your own understanding. In all your ways acknowledge Him, and He will make your paths straight.* (Proverbs 3:5–6)

When our heart produces trust, our mind is empowered to understand in the way that God requires for that particular moment. If our heart does not let us down, then we always have confidence before God (see 1 John 3:21). What our heart imagines under the Holy Spirit, our faith can realize.

> *But just as it is written, "THINGS WHICH EYE HAS NOT SEEN AND EAR HAS NOT HEARD, AND which HAVE NOT ENTERED THE HEART OF MAN, ALL THAT GOD HAS PREPARED FOR THOSE WHO LOVE HIM." For to us God revealed them through the Spirit; for the Spirit searches all things, even the depths of God.* (1 Corinthians 2:9–10)

What God has prepared for us cannot be seen or heard until it has entered our heart. Our inner man is enlightened and then we see the purpose of God and we are opened to hearing on a deeper level. Our identity is out of alignment with God's essential nature until we see Him as He is. He builds everything out of what we have seen.

When Jesus asked the question "Whom do people say that the Son of Man is?" He was essentially asking, "How do they see or perceive me?" What you think about God is the most important thing in the world. That perception is driven by what you see that He is for you. Simon Peter received a spiritual perception of Jesus that changed his name and his personal identity (see Matthew 16:13–20). When we fail to see, then our identity is out of harmony with God's perception of us and our inheritance will be unclaimed.

This is the most vital part of prophecy. When we prophesy, we encourage people to see who they are in Christ. We restore them to an affair of the heart. We build up their confidence and their ability to know the heart and mind of God. All prophetic people are ambassadors of reconciliation, restoring people to their rightful identity. Prophecy restores the heart.

A lifestyle of heart-led responsiveness to the Holy Spirit is the essence of the prophetic gift and ministry. This type of sensitivity to God's name and nature is the heartbeat of prophecy. Approaching the heart of God in prophecy is therefore about ruling in life through the heart.

YOUR PERCEPTION IS LINKED TO YOUR DESTINY

We recognize that our heart is the door that Jesus is knocking on continually (see Revelation 3:20). When we open that door in each situation, then we have an experience of God in fellowship that is ongoing and powerful in its intimate nature.

Our mind is incredible at establishing the truth that our heartfelt experience has opened up to us. Heart and mind working together will enable us to be transformed in life. The issue is that such a paradox is always about primacy. A paradox is two apparently conflicting ideas contained in the same truth, e.g., we have to die to live, give to receive, be last to be first. These are all paradoxes—opposing truths acting out of alignment, not competition. The church is both a body (fluid, changing, flexible) and a building (rigid, unchanging, inflexible). The church is both/and, not either/or. The description of the apostolic ministry is both agricultural and constructive in metaphor. One is organic; the other is organized. We need both, but the order is critical. We can only build the church by growing people, thus the organic has primacy.

The prophetic gift moves in concert with apostolic purpose and divine intent. The key word in prophecy is always edify. Prophecy takes us from a poor perspective of God and self into a much richer outlook on life so that we are built up in the natural and the spiritual dimension together. All prophecy has its roots in edification, exhortation, and comfort. Words that are hard to say must come from this foundation so that people have the opportunity to be built up in their revelation and experience of God.

We have to come to a place where our spirit is a witness to what God is saying. Then we can release our mind to fall in line behind the word, begin the process of understanding it, and eventually speak it out. Our minds will often clash with the revelation we have received. It will try to constrain us, telling us not to speak out the word we have heard. It may seem illogical. To combat that, we need to learn to move in the peace and relaxation of God. We prophesy as far as our faith will allow us to.

SOUL AND SPIRIT

It is very important that we understand the discipline of how to live with God because everything flows out of our relationship with Him. What we think about God is the single most important thing in the world — it is the revelation that will drive our life and provide the channel through which our prophetic gift and ministry will flow.

YOUR WILL IS THE VEHICLE FOR THE SPIRIT

We are probably all aware that man is essentially two parts: soul/body and spirit—what the Bible often calls "the outer man" and "the inner man." In God's design, He intended the Holy Spirit to dwell and mingle with our spirit.

The soul is made up of mind, emotions, and will, and must take its instruction and authority from the Spirit of God. In Scripture, it is spoken of frequently as being something over which we have to gain and exercise authority. *"Therefore we do not lose heart,"* Paul wrote in 2 Corinthians 4:16. *"Even though our outward man is perishing, yet the inward man is being renewed day by day."* Up until the time of salvation, our soul rules unopposed in our life. We live a life unconnected with our spirit until God intervenes. We make our own decisions, reigning and ruling through our soul. We do what we want, living to please ourselves most of the time. We become self-centered and our love is often conditional.

At the moment of salvation, our spirit comes to life but our whole ability to live that life for other people or for ourselves is still dominated by the soul. At salvation, an internal battle begins. God breaks in, we are born again, and our spirit is revitalized. Now the battle for supremacy begins.

There is a law that emerges within us at the moment of salvation. Salvation is not a one-off occurrence—we have been saved, we are being saved, and we will be saved. Salvation is a process of sanctification. Sanctification is about bringing everything within us under the rule of God so that joyfully, in everything that we are and have, we are becoming His. The spirit begins to exert this pressure from within, but the soul doesn't want to give up its rule over us.

If our will is not the vehicle for the spirit, then our emotions will try to run the show. However, our will has an insatiable appetite to be in the presence of God, so our will is the vehicle for life in the spirit, not our mind and emotions. As our will comes under the rule of the spirit, our soul learns how to submit joyfully to the Holy Spirit.[1]

When our soul power is broken, we come into extreme joy. The soul power has to be broken or we cannot serve God effectively. The soul, if unconquered, is always affected by external things. So life in the spirit is about learning how to live from the inside to the outside, not the other way around.

When we live in our soul, we are always waiting for God to do something. When we learn how to live in our spirit, we are our own revival. When we learn how to live in the spirit, we don't need a move of God coming from outside; we have one on the inside of us. This is what Jesus meant when He told the Samaritan woman at the well, "If you drink My water, you'll never have to be thirsty again."

TONGUES

Speaking in tongues, for those people who have the gift, is a very important part of our devotional life and our relationship with God because it edifies our spirit and renews our mind. I love tongues because I can pour out my heart to God in whatever situation I'm in, even if I'm in pain or I'm exhausted. I have an expectation that when I speak in tongues, God will break in and do something. I don't want to use this gift unless I have expectation, for I know that the two go together.

---

[1] For a fuller explanation and impartation of this particular discipline regarding soul and spirit, please read the journal *Towards a Powerful Inner Life*, available at www.brilliantbookhouse.com.

There are times when I want to have ten minutes of adoration of Jesus, where I can sit quietly and pour out my heart about how much He means to me. When we enter that time of praise, our reactions to the circumstances around us change. We begin to respond to things in a godly manner, revering Jesus. It is the opposite spirit in which the world operates. It is the very essence of Jesus' life: "Pray for those who use you; bless those who persecute you."

How do we know that we are being led by the Spirit? The only effective way is by gauging our reactions to situations around us. If something difficult is happening and our reaction is one of peace, joy, thankfulness, gentleness, and humility, we are being led by the Spirit. If what comes out of our mouth is something altogether different, chances are we are being led by the flesh. We know we are being led by the Spirit of God by the kind of character that we are manifesting in given situations. Moving in the opposite spirit is very, very important to us, and of extreme importance to God. Speaking in tongues builds up a reservoir inside of us, helping us to top off the well within. It keeps us unblocked and in communion with God.

UNCEASING PRAYER

Prayer is absolutely vital in our preparation to prophesy. Prayer and prophecy are inextricably linked in terms of the communication process. Both involve listening before talking. In my own prayer time, I usually find myself somewhere in the spiritual paradox between wonderful and frustrating, joyful and pained, confident and uncertain, anointed and unanointed. Fortunately, all of those feelings are the same to God:

PRAY WITH GOD — NOT TOWARD HIM!

prayer is prayer. When my daughter was thirteen, she described prayer perfectly to me: "Some days, you get in the elevator and zoom to the penthouse suite. Other days, you take the stairs." Either way, prayer is an interesting journey.

Most of us don't listen enough before we pray. When I pray something, I listen straight away, just in case God tells me I can have what I asked for. Sometimes we pray more than we need to because we never hear God say yes. Wherever we pray, whatever we pray, we must get into a habit of immediately listening.

Often, we listen best when we are reading. If that's the case, we ought to read the Bible before an extended, set-apart time of prayer. The Holy Spirit can and will impress on us something from Scripture. Perhaps God gave us two ears and one mouth so we would listen twice as much as talk.

Prayer, in its simplest form, is finding out what God wants to do and then asking Him to do it. When we don't listen before we pray, we end up presenting God with options instead of a request. We'll pray whatever comes to mind instead of entering into communion with Him. Our internal, clamoring agenda gives God a multiple choice prayer. "Please, Lord, do *A*. Unless *B* is Your will. Or *C*. But *D* would be great, too," we pray. By practicing stillness and communicating with Him throughout the day, we can better hear and understand His heart for our issues.

Prayer is praying with God, not to God. It is praying with the answer, not to try to find one.[2]

God is very different from us. God is always still and often silent, but He punctuates that silence with words. This makes every word God

---

[2] For a fuller explanation of this joyful discipline, please read the journal on Crafted Prayer available at www.brilliantbookhouse.com.

JOHN G. LAKE

Lived: 1870 to 1935

Prophetic Synopsis: Surrounded by death and illness all his life (eight of his fifteen siblings died young), Lake was desperate for God to heal. In the 1890s, Lake heard about John Dowie's healing rooms and took his brother to one: the man was healed. Later, he took his sister, who suffered from cancer, to Dowie. She was healed too. In 1896, Lake's wife, Jennie, contracted tuberculosis, and she was healed as well.

Ten years later, after seasons of prayer and fasting and being mentored by Dowie, Lake prayed for a woman with rheumatism. God filled the room and His power fell on Lake like warm rain. He heard the Lord say to him, "I have heard your prayers. I have seen your tears. You are now baptized in the Holy Spirit." The woman was healed.

The Lakes went to South Africa and planted more than 600 churches. When Jennie died, John returned to America and settled in Spokane, Washington, opening a series of healing rooms.

In six years in Spokane, 100,000 healings took place—that's forty-five every day! A Washington, D.C., doctor declared Spokane the healthiest city in the world. A Better Business Bureau committee investigated one hundred healings and concluded, "We soon found out... you did not tell the half of it."

Lake could put his hands on a person and the Holy Spirit would show him what was wrong. He could go into a hospital, speak to a patient whose condition baffled doctors, pray, and discern exactly what their ailment was.

Key Comment: "The currents of power began to rush through my being from the crown of my head to the soles of my feet."

Sources: Stanley Burgess and Gary McGee, editors *Dictionary of Pentecostal and Charismatic Movements* (Grand Rapids, MI: Zondervan, 1996). Roberts Liardon, *God's Generals* (Tulsa, OK: Albury Publishing, 1996).

speaks an event, because He has an inherent creativity in the power of His Word. In Genesis 1:3, He said, *"Let there be light,"* and there was light for the first time. His first recorded message was an incredible event, and one sung about for thousands of years after — *"By the word of the LORD the heavens were made,"* says Psalm 33:6. John 1:1–5 gives another glimpse of the creative power of God's word:

> *In the beginning was the Word, and the Word was with God, and the Word was God. He was in the beginning with God. All things were made through Him, and without Him nothing was made that was made. In Him was life, and the life was the light of men. And the light shines in the darkness, and the darkness did not comprehend it.*

Human beings, on the other hand, punctuate words with silence. We're always talking and rarely quiet. This makes our silence an event. We're usually quiet only for the purposes of reflection, or if we're searching something out.

The great thing about God is that He doesn't have to talk to communicate. Just a look can be sufficient. The Bible says that Jesus turned and looked at Peter and broke his heart. God can speak to us through His love, His joy, and even His presence. We just have to carve out time to spend in that quiet place with Him. The more disciplined we become in every moment of our lives, the more dialogue we will engage Him in.

A discipline does not have to be a heavy or onerous duty. It is a joy if we choose to see it that way. It describes a joyful routine that does our hearts good—like brushing our teeth in the morning or our first sip of coffee each day.

All daily routines need to be joyful, otherwise the stress of it can unbalance our approach to life. The Holy Spirit is so brilliant at playing the enjoyment game; it is what makes fellowship with Him a complete delight!

Before the Lord called me into my current ministry, I was the business development manager for a large training and recruitment company. My life was a hectic round of business deals, management problems, employment research, government negotiations, training sessions, event organizing, and strategic oversight.

> **SPIRITUAL DISCIPLINE IS A JOYFUL ROUTINE THAT DOES OUR HEART GOOD**

There were times in those busy days when I would tell my secretarial staff that I needed ten minutes of undisturbed rest. I would retreat into my office, close the door, and sit quietly, thanking God, listening to Him, asking Him for His perspective, and praying for His help. Many right decisions came out of those short bursts of prayer. While I can't say I always heard God specifically in those moments (although sometimes I did), He did shape me in those times. My track record at the company, together with my continuous promotion among the staff, indicates that the Lord influenced me far more than I actually knew. Those prayer times kept my heart free from ungodly pressure—they were like a spiritual lifeline for me.

Prayer can come in seasons. When I wrote *Developing Your Prophetic Gifting* all those years ago, I was in a season of my life where God answered many of my prayers immediately. What once took days or weeks to be prayed through suddenly took minutes. I was learning to hear God more clearly, and my expectation in terms of listening grew. My prayers were full of faith because I knew God was listening and acting.

Obviously, prayer is not just about being in request mode before God. He isn't Santa Claus, after all. The wonderful thing about prayer is that we can talk to God about anything and everything, wherever we are, whatever we're thinking, or whatever we're feeling. We have the freedom to open up our spirit and go places with God. I specialize in short prayers: "Lord, help this person," I'll ask Him during the day. "Father, remember my friends out there in Africa," I say. I keep the flow of prayer going, holding open a channel of communication between the two of us. The best way for someone to enter the secret place with God is to never leave it. By stepping back into our inner man and working at being peaceful and restful, we can develop deep, constant communication with Him.

A life of unceasing prayer allows us to continuously talk everything through as it comes into our lives. We can mention things to God immediately and constantly. It happens conversationally; we just run the things in our heart by God, as we would a good friend. Our fears, our shortcomings, our hopes, our dreams, our concerns, and our joys can all be brought to God in unceasing prayer.

Such a lifestyle releases our soul to be at peace because we have committed to God everything that is happening in our lives. He has a stake in all of it. Our spirit—the part of us that communicates with God—influences our soul positively when we engage with God constantly. When we talk about every situation with God, things are put into an eternal context. It makes us less prone to anxiety, worry, fear, and idle speculation. Instead, we are watching for God to do something incredible in, and through, us. The apostle John knew this principle, and instructed us in it in 1 John 5:14–15:

Now this is the confidence that we have in Him, that if we ask anything according to His will, He hears us. And if we know that He hears us, whatever we ask, we know that we have the petitions that we have asked of Him.

Prayer is a matter of continually asking the Holy Spirit to break in and speak. When was the last time you asked the Lord for some encouragement? If it has been awhile, try it right now. "Father, I need some encouragement. Please would You do something; please would You say something; please help me."

PRAYER, POWER, PROCESS

Living constantly in the presence of God can heal us of our old wounds, and even our physical illnesses. Emotional, spiritual, mental, and physical needs are all the same to the Father. We know that God is able to heal instantly, but there are also occasions when He heals us over a longer period of time. We can be healed both immediately by His power and gradually through our relationship with Him. At times, the Lord is developing our capacity to walk in power and authority. On these occasions, when under the guidance of His will, we pray the prayers of authority and faith and we see immediate results. At these times, too, our prayers are accompanied by a specific gift of faith,

CONFIDENCE IS ROOTED IN WHO GOD IS FOR US NOW

healing, or miracles, and we can be amazed at how heaven comes to Earth in those moments.

Still, there are other times when we enter a process of healing that seems to be in line with God's desire to redevelop our relationship with Him. We are not ill or wounded because our relationship with God lacks depth. God Himself is not mean to us; He does not deny healing for the sake of building relationship. Rather, the Father simply uses what is available to touch and deepen us in difficult moments.

In all our situations, the love of the Father is profound enough to upgrade our image of Him, that we may know His nature and lordship in a more realistic manner.

Healing through relationship is a process because the Lord is developing our patience, endurance, and steadfast trust. It is the keeping power of God that increases our faith and brings us to a new level of perception, relationship, and, ultimately, revelation. He nurtures us as we pray in faith and learn to abide in the shadow of His wings. He does not always deliver us from the valley, but He does always walk through it with us.

God is our keeper and loves His role in watching over us and teaching us to abide in confidence.[3] We learn to trust the Father as we actively listen to the One who ever lives to make intercession for us (see Hebrews 7:25) and learn to walk with the Comforter. It is vital that we allow the Holy Spirit to develop this particular role in our lives. We can be weak and find God's strength through comfort as well as through joy.

---

3 For a fuller understanding of this powerful truth, Graham's Journal on God's Keeping Power would be valuable study on building a relationship with God's intentional nature. Available on www.brilliantbookhouse.com.

In the valley, in the process of restoration, renewal, and finding physical, mental, emotional, or spiritual health, we learn how best to fight. In this instance, the weapons of our warfare are thanksgiving, praise, trust, and rest. Sometimes we inherit the promises of God immediately, but, at other times, it comes through faith and patience.

FREEDOM IS ABOUT ALWAYS BEING FREE!

Even if God's power is not demonstrated immediately, His sovereignty will always come through progressively. Power and process are designed by God's will. If it is process that He chooses to heal us in, we must wait gladly on the Lord and remain attentive to His voice and bound to His loving nature.

Words of knowledge may come through others about our circumstances. Sometimes these words are accompanied by another gift of faith, healing, or miracles, and we are set free. If not, they are God's encouragement for us to continue praying and believing in the process of life. The prophecy may carry the certainty of God's ultimate will, giving us confidence. We can craft them into a prayer to use daily, knowing we are praying God's will and therefore the answer to our dilemma.

Freed from the tyranny of our current condition, we are now released in heart and mind to pursue the other purposes of God in our circumstances. What else does He want to do apart from our ultimate healing? Is our healing a part of our wider restoration and renewal? Is the Lord taking us into a deeper place of abiding love and intimacy? He knows the plans He has for us, in every situation, to give us a future and a hope! What is He planning in that beautiful heart that loves us so amazingly? What grace will come our way? What wisdom and insight may open the eyes of our heart?

This is the path and the process of enlightenment that enables us to fully know God and to be known, as we read in Ephesians 1:15–23. We use what we are exploring and discovering to pray with certainty and to formulate our own psalms of thanksgiving. David's intentional, written-out praise—or as we now call them, the Psalms—were what enabled him to become a man after God's own heart.

INTIMATE PRAYER

A few years ago, God began to speak to me about a new kind of prayer He was about to release to us. Paradoxically, this new method is actually an ancient way of prayer, one in which God's faithful servants like David and Paul flourished. These heroes of the faith learned how to pray exactly what God willed for a person, and they saw His answer unfold before their very eyes. This type of prayer can transform Christians from living in a persistent widow mindset (see Luke 18:1–8) into living in joyous, bride-like intercession.

> **PRAY LIKE A BRIDE, NOT A WIDOW**

As the Bride of Christ, we carry incredible favor with God. This favor is similar to the favor Queen Esther found in the eyes of her king. I believe God is taking many Christians into a new season of intimate, bride-like prayer. Real warfare in the kingdom of God is always concerned with the battle for intimacy. This is a time to come off the battlefield and enter a new place of intimate petition. Many intercessors have become too exhausted and too burned-out to continue praying the way the Church has been advocating. As we learn to become conformed to God and His nature, and be transformed in our minds and personalities, He will teach us to look beyond the natural

KATHRYN KUHLMAN

Lived: 1907 to 1976

Prophetic Synopsis: Separated from her husband, and having just lost her fledgling ministry, Kathryn Kuhlman was desperate for God in the mid 1940s. After praying for several days, she was touched by the Holy Spirit: "Four o'clock that Saturday afternoon, having come to the place in my life where I surrendered everything, I knew nothing about the fullness of the Holy Spirit. I knew nothing about speaking in an unknown tongue. I knew nothing about the deeper truths of the Word," she said. That afternoon, Kathryn Kuhlman died. "If you've never had that death to the flesh, you don't know what I'm talking about. When you're completely filled with the Holy Spirit, when you've had that experience as they had in the upper room, there will be a death to the flesh, believe me. I surrendered unto Him all there was of me, everything! Then for the first time, I realized what it meant to have real power."

Kuhlman's ministry exploded as the power of God followed her everywhere. When a woman was healed of a tumor while she preached, she turned her attention to healing. Hundreds, and then thousands, were healed as she shared the power of the Holy Spirit. She became very gifted in giving words of knowledge regarding illnesses: "How does one know the woman over there in such and such a dress is being healed? I don't know. If my life depended on it, I could not tell you. I do not know but the Holy Spirit knows."

In 1965, Kathryn moved to Los Angeles and held meetings in the Shrine Auditorium. She preached there for ten years, filling the 7,000-seat room almost every night. She became famous. She preached five hundred times on CBS television. Magazines like Redbook, People, Time, and Christianity Today did stories on her. She went on all of the popular talk shows, including Johnny Carson, Mike Douglas, Merv Griffin, and Dinah Shore. She met movie stars, singers, TV actors, and even Pope Paul VI.

Key Comment: "His power is under His authority—not ours."

Sources: Stanley Burgess and Gary McGee, editors *Dictionary of Pentecostal and Charismatic Movements* (Grand Rapids, MI: Zondervan, 1996). Roberts Liardon, *God's Generals* (Tulsa, OK: Albury Publishing, 1996).

into the supernatural realm and see the kingdom of heaven at work in every need. It will no longer matter what life, people, or even the enemy throws at us, because we will understand that God is at work all around us.

I believe God is raising up an army of Esthers, an army of bridal intercessors, and it is a time to come off the wall and rest in the throne room presence of God—in our secret place in Him. It will be difficult for some people to come out of ministry and move into the discipline of resting in God, but the discipline of rest must be entered. This is a time of laying down ministry to gain fresh intimacy.

Don't pray with importunity, like the widow before the unjust judge in Luke 18, but pray with delight and favor. Don't just pray against the enemy, but also let your delighted prayers cause the King to stir Himself and come down. God's anointing will cause you to intercede with joy so that His glory will fill the earth. What is the glory of God? In Exodus 33:18–19, when Moses asked God to show His glory, God said He would cause His goodness to pass before him. One of the glories of God, therefore, is that He is good!

BEGGING IS NOT FAVOR!

As bridal intercessors, it will be our joy and delight to pray for the goodness of God to come down so that the Church can learn that we really do overcome evil with good. The Holy Spirit will give us a new strategy for prayer and perseverance—one that contains delight and laughter and is full of ardent and passionate love, bathed in fresh worship, and birthed out of a deeper intimacy.

As we come and petition the Lord out of this place of closeness, He will be pleased to speak His favor and blessing into our hearts. Not only will our prayers move His heart and hands, but the words we receive from Him will be like a balm of Gilead across the nations, and churches will rise up in fresh favor. The attention of the Church will be taken off the enemy and put on God.

PURSUE LOVE

Historically, the biggest failure in the prophetic has been a lack of love in prophets' hearts. In 1 Corinthians 14:1–5, the apostle Paul addressed that very shortcoming:

Pursue love, and desire spiritual gifts, but especially that you may prophesy. For he who speaks in a tongue does not speak to men but to God, for no one understands him; however, in the spirit he speaks mysteries. But he who prophesies speaks edification and exhortation and comfort to men. He who speaks in a tongue edifies himself, but he who prophesies edifies the church. I wish you all spoke with tongues, but even more that you prophesied; for he who prophesies is greater than he who speaks with tongues, unless indeed he interprets, that the church may receive edification.

"*Pursue love,*" Paul said. That's the best piece of advice I can give anyone seeking to move in the prophetic: pursue love. Most people, when they're learning about prophecy, jump into the Old Testament first, looking at how the great prophets prophesied. However, a huge difference exists between the Old Testament and New Testament styles.

In New Testament prophecy, it is vital that we pursue God for all we're worth. God is love, therefore we cannot pursue God if we do not pursue love. "*Beloved, let us love one another, for love is of God; and everyone who loves is born of God and knows God,"* says 1 John 4:7. When we pursue God with all our heart, one thing should be happening—we should become more and more in love with loving the people around us.

Our heart will be changed to accept everyone, even people we previously couldn't stand being around. *"Love your enemies, do good to those who hate you, bless those who curse you, and pray for those who spitefully use you,"* Jesus taught in Luke 6:27–28. Even more astonishing than His teaching was the fact that He did just that: He loved people who hated Him. *"Father, forgive them, for they do not know what they do,"* He prayed in Luke 23:34 as the men crucifying Him cast lots for His clothing. If we are pursuing God, everybody around us is a potential target for God's love. No one is safe from the love of God.

TO PURSUE LOVE IS TO BE CAUGHT BY IT FIRST!

The reason God put us in the circle of people we're with in our workplace, neighborhood, and church, is so that He can pour out His love through us. And the nastier they are, the more God wants us to love them.

In the prophetic, love needs to be our foundation. There is nothing worse—and I know this from experience—than being in a roomful of people, all of whom are waiting for a prophetic word, and you haven't got any love in your heart. It is a lonely, awful place to be. Most of the prophets I know who have had nervous breakdowns have done so because they had no real depth of love for people in their heart.

The only pressure we ought to be under is the pressure to be loved by God and to love others. I have found that the safest place to be in ministry. When I am surrounded by the expectancy of hundreds of people, and I have nothing to say, and I don't know what God wants

EVAN ROBERTS

Lived: 1878 to 1951

Prophetic Synopsis: At age twenty, Roberts had a prophetic vision that changed his life. In it, he saw the moon, full and bright, with an arm stretching from it into Wales. Immediately, he knew that God was about to touch his country, bringing 100,000 people to the faith.

It wasn't just visions Roberts experienced. One Friday night, he had been deep in prayer: "It was communion with God," he said. "Before this I was afar off from God. I was frightened that night, but never since. So great was my shivering that I rocked the bed, and my brother, being wakened, took hold of me, thinking I was ill."

Roberts had another powerful vision, just before the Welsh Revival hit: "I had a vision of all Wales being lifted up to Heaven. We are going to see the mightiest revival Wales has ever known—the Holy Ghost is coming soon, so we must get ready."

He was right; God used him to move in Wales in a powerful way. Thousands were healed. Roberts's prophetic gift became so finely tuned that he could tell the nonbelievers in a room and preach directly to them. "The revival in south Wales is not of men, but of God," he said. "He has come very close to us. I have been asked concerning my methods. I have none. I never prepare what I shall speak, but I leave that to Him. I am not the source of the revival, but only one servant among what is growing to be a multitude. I wish no personal following, but only the world for Christ. I believe the world is on the threshold of a great religious revival, and pray daily that I may be allowed to help bring this about."

Just as he prophesied, 100,000 Welsh people came to Christ in six months.

Key Comment: "Ask and it shall be given unto you. Practice entire, definite faith in God's promise of the Spirit."

Sources: Stanley Burgess and Gary McGee, editors, *Dictionary of Pentecostal and Charismatic Movements* (Grand Rapids, MI: Zondervan, 1996). Roberts Liardon, *God's Generals* (Tulsa, OK: Albury Publishing, 1996).

to do next, being loved by Him creates a peace inside myself. It is a safe environment because all I can do is stand there and let God love me.

To be successful long-term in ministry, we have to understand how to be loved by God. When God's love touches a human being, it changes things on the inside. We can only pursue what has apprehended us. God made love His first commandment because it is His biggest value. He commands us to love because He commands it of Himself. He demands what He most wants to give. It takes God to love God. Only God can love God well. He gives to us first the very thing He most wants from us. *"We love Him because He first loved us"* (1 John 4:19). Our chief delight is to respond to the love of God and to return it to Him.

Everything originates in God (see John 3:27), therefore everything comes from Him; it runs through Him and goes back to Him (see Romans 11:35–36). What God commands, He is first to bestow. His initiative draws our response. Love is always available.

Everyone aspiring to move in the prophetic must have their hearts conditioned by love. Learning to be loved on a daily basis is our biggest lesson. Accepting and allowing the love of God to penetrate our heart, soul, mind, and physical strength is a lifelong pleasure. To be still in His love. To rest in His love. To find joy and delight in God's loving nature. To be wrapped in His love and the majesty of His grace. To be free to give love to anyone, regardless of circumstances.

To speak from the platform of God's love is an awesome pleasure and a very real responsibility. The chief role of a prophet is to make God radiant in His people. My prime ministry after worship is simply to reach Christians for Christ. As prophetic people, our experience of God's love makes us aware of what He is doing in the hearts of those we minister to. God puts us between His heart and someone else's, and we can become a conduit for God's love to flow to someone. Love teaches us to see what God is seeing, to feel what God is feeling, to bless what God is blessing, and to do what God is doing.

NEW BEGINNINGS

Prophecy can restore people's dignity and self-respect. It can give them hope again. But to do this, we must be steeped in God's love. We are either living in the present/past or the present/future in our relationship with the Lord and one another. Some relationships are stuck in the past because they are connected to memories and encounters that were either traumatic or eventful.

Our mind and emotions play the same tapes over and over until it becomes a normal part of our background conversation. Current mindsets have been overcome by memory. It is our head noise that ruins the present. Some of our memories can be wonderful and yet can still keep our relationships in the past if we have not upgraded them for some time. The phrase "we must catch up one day" is one that we all use to signify that our relationship needs to become more current.

The best relationships have a present to future application—a "now" and "not yet" feel that provides the sense of a shared journey, an exploration of life. We live in the present with a strong sense of our and others potential. We are all a mix of visible traits and hidden capabilities.

GOD IS PRESENT-FUTURE IN HIS RELATIONSHIP WITH US

The latter may only emerge when the proper circumstances arise. Until then they are dormant and may only be recognized by the prophetic.

The Father lives with us and occupies the space between the potential we have and the actual that He views in our future. A prophecy is spoken from the future back to the present. That does not yet make it real or substantial. Free will is involved. Prophecy relates to the possibility, not the inevitability of fulfillment, because the will of the individual/group has to be engaged in cooperation with the Lord in order for the word to come to pass. "Be it unto me according to your word" is a sure sign that Mary fully intended to cooperate with the Father regarding the birth of Jesus.

Sometimes people are trapped into reliving or reenacting their past in current relationships. Prophetic ministry needs to enter that place gently, lovingly, and firmly to extricate the individual from a present/past lifestyle. Prophecy in this context has an objective to restore people's dignity and self-respect.

The best way to extricate people from the past is first to show them their future. Everyone has to have something to reach for in life.

> *Not that I have already obtained it or have already become perfect, but I press on so that I may lay hold of that for which also I was laid hold of by Christ Jesus. Brethren, I do not regard myself as having laid hold of it yet; but one thing I do: forgetting what lies behind and reaching forward to what lies ahead, I press on toward the goal for the prize of the upward call of God in Christ Jesus. Let us therefore, as many as are perfect, have this attitude; and if in anything you have a different attitude, God will reveal that also to you; however, let us keep living by that same standard to which we have attained. (Philippians 3:12–16)*

MARIA WOODWORTH-ETTER

Lived: 1844 to 1924

Prophetic Synopsis: Maria Woodworth-Etter was barely a teenager when God spoke to her: "I heard the voice of Jesus calling me to go out in the highways and hedges and gather in the lost sheep." Still, Maria married a man who did not believe in women in ministry. Five of their six children died young, even as God continually called Maria to preach.

All of the death and all of the wrestling with God pushed Maria into the Bible. She read every word, trying to find some meaning for her life. As she read, she saw examples of women—like Mary, Deborah, Esther, Miriam, Hulda, Anna, Priscilla, and others—being used by God to do unbelievable things.

One day, Maria looked up from the Bible and prayed: "Lord, I can't preach. I don't know what to say and I don't have any education." At that instant, God gave her a vision that electrified her life: "I thought I would go through a course of study and prepare for work, thinking the Lord would make my husband and people willing in some way to let me go out and work... The dear Saviour stood by me one night in a vision and talked to me face to face... Jesus said 'You can tell people what the Lord has done for your soul; tell of the glory of God and the love of Jesus.'"

Woodworth-Etter did exactly that. At age thirty-five, she began her ministry, preaching, prophesying, and healing the sick. She was famous for falling into Spirit-induced trances while speaking. She would simply stop moving, and God's presence would fill the room as people waited for her to "come to." Her gift of healing was so incredible that she was twice charged with practicing medicine without a licence.

Key Comment: "Let us not plead weakness; God will use the weak things of the world to confuse the wise. We are sons and daughters of the Most High God. Should we not honour our high calling and do all we can to save those who sit in the valley and shadow of death?"

Sources: Stanley Burgess and Gary McGee, editors, *Dictionary of Pentecostal and Charismatic Movements* (Grand Rapids, MI: Zondervan, 1996). Roberts Liardon, *God's Generals* (Tulsa, OK: Albury Publishing, 1996).

Pressing on is made more possible through the influx of prophecy.

People need to forget the past. *"The former things have passed away, now I declare new things. Before they spring forth, I proclaim them to you"* (Isaiah 42:9).

PROPHECY IS THE LANGUAGE OF PROMISE REVEALED

The prophetic must put us in mind of a future time in regard to our present. When our mind is able to cover the ground between our present and the future, then we are free to move on in the things of God. If our mind is only backtracking to the past, there can be no momentum.

"Do not call to mind the former things or ponder things of the past. Behold I will do something new, now it will spring forth. Will you not be aware of it?" (Isaiah 43:18–19).

Prophecy makes us aware of the future and it therefore has the capacity to call us up and out of something.

Prophecy can put us in touch with the romantic part of God's nature regarding His love for His bride who is the beloved of His heart. Prophecy calls us to the next stage of life and the next phase of relationship with our Beloved Jesus.

> *My beloved responded and said to me, "Arise, my darling, my beautiful one, and come along. For behold, the winter is past, the rain is over and gone. The flowers have already appeared in the land; the time has arrived for pruning the vines, and the voice of the turtledove has been heard in our land. The fig tree has ripened its figs, and the vines in blossom have given forth their fragrance. Arise, my darling, my beautiful one, and come along!"* (Song of Solomon 2:10–13)

It carries the language of promise. You need to love moving to the next chapter of your experience. Hard times are over and new things are appearing. The Lord leaves us in no doubt of His affection for us. This is so much the heart of all true prophecy. The restoring of dignity and self-respect is essential to the individual moving into a stronger relationship as the beloved of God. Prophecy causes us to arise and come away into a deeper relationship as the beloved. The Lord wears His heart on His sleeve, always visible, always tangible. He is so tactile in His affection for us.

When people have been damaged, it is the future that can release them from the past. The present is merely rerunning memory tapes and is therefore more prone to repeating scenarios from the past. The future alone calls people up to a new beginning. Prophecy tells us that God is with us (present) and also moving in advance of us (future). He will help us. He will deliver us. He will not fail us.

The LORD is the one who goes ahead of you; He will be with you He will not fail you or forsake you. Do not fear or be dismayed. (Deuteronomy 31:8)

There is always a new you emerging! The Father loves to change us from one degree of glory to another. His love for us is transformational. He loves to create new from old. He is astonishingly brilliant at the process of transformation. He uses prophecy to create movement and momentum to take us out of the Egypt of our current circumstances into and the Canaan of His promise and affection.

ONLY THE FUTURE CAN RELEASE US FROM THE PAST!

Prophetic people have this same affection and excitement in their heart. It shows in how they view people, in the message of hope they carry, and in the way they present that message and deliver the heart of the Lord. What an amazing gift is prophecy! What an amazing burden the Lord wants to give us. It is a burden, a passion for freedom and to see God's beloved becoming more captivated by His deep love and longing.

Prophetic input is an invaluable aid in the development of our identity. What is emerging in you right now? Who are you becoming? We all change. Prophecy provides us with the means to connect ourselves to the heart of God regarding our future and our destiny. It provides continuity in the affection of God. "I am with you always." No matter how the road ahead may challenge the journey, the Lord is unchangeable toward us. He is a constant, our North Star.

THREE PHASES OF REVELATION

Generally, there are three parts to revelation. A word of knowledge often opens people up, while a prophetic word fills the gap created. Finally, a word of wisdom can give instruction on what to do next. These three elements work together to form the broader prophetic gifting.

A word of knowledge is simply revelation about something that has happened that the prophet could have no way of knowing, except supernaturally through the Holy Spirit. Sometimes, a word of knowledge can lift people right out of the pit of despair. On other occasions, God uses it to build a series of steps so people can walk out of the pit themselves. It is the

PROPHECY IS NOT JUST WHAT WE SAY BUT HOW WE SAY IT

prophet's job to know the difference and to know what God wants to do in the word of knowledge He gives us.

Words of knowledge, because they are so personal, can be intensely powerful. I remember prophesying over a man named Michael. God gave me a burden for him, but he was a complete wall. I was breaking up on the inside, but he looked like he was totally together.

"Father," I prayed internally, "what's the best way of speaking to this man's wall? If I just give him a word, it will rebound off of him. How do I reach him?"

Almost immediately, I felt the Holy Spirit tell me to ask him about his dad. I put my hand on Michael's shoulder and asked him about his father. Suddenly, unexpectedly, almost unbelievably, the wall fell. Michael choked with tears and began to sob. It was as if God pressed a button in his heart, one only He knew existed.

"Michael," I said, "I have a picture of you when you were six years old. Your dad made a kite for you. He made it in his shed at the bottom of your garden and he spent a long time on it. Your dad was a perfectionist and he gave you the kite for your birthday. It wasn't really what you wanted but you liked it. Still, your response wasn't what he wanted — he wanted you to be excited about it after all the hours he had put into it. You went outside to try it, but you were kind of clumsy as a child. I see you tripping over your own feet and putting a hole through the kite. Your dad was livid; he stood you up against a wall and began to tell you a number of negative statements." I recounted some of those phrases to him and watched as he completely broke down. The dam had broken in his life through the word of knowledge.

At that point, people around us began to jump in with words of encouragement and scripture that fit with what I was saying. I quieted them down because I knew there was more God wanted to take hold of. Sometimes, in our humanity, we want to rebuild a person too quickly. When there's a crack in a wall, God may want to scoop more than just the surface out. Prophetic people need to look at the whole battle, not just the first shot.

After a few minutes, Michael began to calm down. During that time, I had been praying and asking God what He wanted to do next. At the age of six, a curse had been put on this man's life. Being a victim as a child followed him into adulthood.

I then had a second word of knowledge for Michael. I saw him in a room with three other men. These men were all shaking their fingers at him, telling him, "You've missed it; you're out of the will of God; you're going to lose your way; you're going to be ineffective."

The Lord showed me that he had been part of a leadership team that disagreed about what they felt God was calling them to do. The three men didn't want to go where Michael was suggesting. The men wanted to play it safe; Michael wanted to take a risk for Christ. My heart went out to him. While God is completely safe as far as His character and love go, He is a risk-taker in vision. He is not safe in who He calls or what He wants to do. He asks us to accomplish the impossible.

In that instant, God showed me how He wanted to reach out to Michael.

"Michael, God wants you to know you haven't missed it," I whispered to him. "Those three men were wrong. What they told you four years ago was wrong. God says, 'Son, you haven't missed it.'" This time, the dam burst at an even greater level. We almost needed to mop the floor, he cried so hard. As he wept

TRUE PROPHECY BINDS UP THE ENEMY, NOT PEOPLE

and wept, I turned him over to the people who had words of affirmation and comfort.

Prophets must listen to the heartbeat of God at all times. We can never assume that He is finished working in a person. God loves to lavish His love on people, pouring Himself into them. What He wants is for us to pursue love for each person we meet. We are not called to pursue our own gifting or ministry, but to pursue the love of God for ourselves and other people. By learning how to be sensitive to the Holy Spirit, we learn how to be sensitive to those around us.

After finishing with Michael, we felt that God wanted to do something in the rest of his family. We asked Marion, his wife, to come up to the stage. The whole room was euphoric—they could see and feel the presence of God. After the two words of knowledge for Michael, I knew logically that his wife would have suffered with him through the past several years. It wasn't prophetic; it was common sense.

I asked God if there was anything He wanted to help her through. The time with Michael had been so powerful that my spirit was wide open to what God was saying. His whisper felt like a shout in my bones. He showed me that twelve years before, she had a traumatic experience while giving birth to their only child. She had severe post-natal depression, went through a period of mental instability, and had spent eight years on medication. Plus she had problems with her self-image. To be honest, that was more than I wanted to know. What could I do with that kind of information? I couldn't just relay it and totally humiliate the woman. It would have destroyed her.

"What do I do, Father?" I prayed. "How do I handle this?" In my heart, I knew it was important that she speak because she was going to have to be part of the process of healing. God wanted to bring healing to the very roots of who she was.

"Marion," I said carefully, "that was a really traumatic birth you had twelve years ago, wasn't it?" She began to cry almost immediately. I asked the Lord to show me how she was feeling so I could put things in a way that would release her, not shatter her. "God knows how you felt at the time—alone, frightened, misunderstood. You couldn't break out of the spiral you were in. Lots of people prayed for you and gave you scriptures, prophesies, and when you didn't get any better, they blamed it on the demonic."

It was like peeling an onion; every layer brought her closer and closer to healing. I kept away from the issues that would have humiliated her, but she knew that God knew them. The people around her hadn't understood her pain. They had judged her based on the surface instead of getting inside the pain she had felt.

That day, all I did was what those Christians around her should have done all those years before—asked God to let me inside her pain: the loss of knowing her first child would be her last and the grief of being misunderstood and judged.

"Do you think you could let go of all that?" I asked her. "Could you forgive the people who didn't understand?" She began to forgive, even as I asked God for a word of prophecy. Until that point, I had been operating out of the word of knowledge. Now I wanted to see if God had something for her future.

PROPHECY CONFIRMS WHAT GOD HAS DONE, IS DOING, AND WILL DO!

"I want you to tell her she was healed four years ago," the Lord said to me.

"Really?" I replied. "What do You mean?"

"The enemy has robbed her of her healing for four years," He said. "She has been healed—she just has to acknowledge the truth."

"Okay," I said. "How did You heal her?"

"I healed her when those men blasted her husband," God explained. "He went right down the tubes for almost nine months and was completely depressed. She saw the pain and grief he was going through and made a conscious decision to take herself off the tranquilizers. She ran the house again, kept everything in line, prayed, and was a strong partner to him during that awful period. I allowed some things to happen in her husband's life because it was the point where his wife was healed. But she has been under this low self-esteem for so long that she has never acknowledged the fact she is doing well. From the day her husband began to slide, she has carried the family. Graham, she doesn't need prayer for healing; she needs to be told, 'You're healed, and this is the evidence.'"

I looked at her and said, "Marion, God has given me a word for you." As I recounted what God had shown me, the lights went on in her mind like they do when one enters a dark house and flips a switch. She finally saw the evidence of God's healing.

"The enemy has got a part of your mind convinced that nothing has happened," I said, "but the reality of your life bears out something much different."

A grin spread across Marion's face as her spirit witnessed to what God was saying.

"Yeah, yeah, you're right," she said. "I am healed." At that precise moment, things broke loose in the spiritual realm. She was healed by acknowledging the truth of what the enemy had hid from her. She was delivered and restored. Suddenly, she had all of the power, strength, worth, and value in the world. Scales dropped from her eyes and she could see that God had done something incredible.

The prophetic is not about the prophet but about God and putting His love into people's hearts. We must never parade what we know in the spirit. The essential quality after love that we need is humility — a desire to have only Christ be seen in us. Prophets must think through their styles and find one that does not distract from the power of God's message. Sensitivity to the Lord is the basis for all prophecy.

OPERATING IN PROPHECY

Having a desire to prophesy is half the battle, as Paul taught in 1 Corinthians 14:1 — *"Pursue love, and desire spiritual gifts, especially that you may prophesy."* In some situations, I have been tired or hungry and not in the mood to prophesy. At those moments, I have heard God tell me to "stir up my spirit."

"I'm tired," I say.

"Son, have a desire, because if you have a desire, I can work," He answers. Before I know it, I have forgotten about the fatigue and I am doing what God wants. We need to look for prophecy, expecting and wanting it to be a part of our lives.

Desire leads us to the next attitude every prophet needs: expectancy. If we are going to move in any spiritual gift, we need to have a sense of expectation. I expect God to do something today. I don't want to live an hour without expectation. There is nothing worse than realizing, on Friday night, that we have drifted through a whole week without having a meaningful conversation or moment with God. When I wake up in the morning, I want to have an expectation that God is going to do something that very day.

Expectation is all-important. The heroes of the faith listed in this book all expected God to do something with them. Expectation was the common thread in all of their lives, even though their ministries spanned two millennia and a dozen different cultures. They believed God would speak to them, and through them, every day.

Expectancy is the lifeblood of moving in the Spirit. We are all pregnant with purpose. When we live as divine carriers of the life of Christ, we develop an attitude, a mindset, and a heart response that flow from that inner life source.

The secret place of our spirit always acts as a womb to birth in us the seed of the next part of our life journey and ministry. What new thing is growing in you today? What partnership with the Holy Spirit is required to bring that expectation to full term and delivery?

Several years ago, I believe the Lord spoke to me about moving in the gift of prophecy every day. He was trying to grow in me a greater expectation in the Holy Spirit. I haven't been perfect in that call, but the practice of expectancy has sharpened the gift and broadened my vision for the prophetic considerably.

> **MOVE IN WHAT YOU HAVE PERMISSION FOR AND PREPARE FOR THE NEXT THING GOD IS BIRTHING IN YOU!**

When I want to move in prophecy, I believe that God can speak into a situation. I expect God to speak into a person's life. This leads into the next step in operating in the prophecy: believing that God is going to speak through us. "Lord, anoint my eyes, ears, and mouth," we pray. With our minds, we should believe we have the mind of Christ, as Paul wrote in 1 Corinthians 2:16. If I have the choice, I want to dismantle my way of thinking and adopt God's instead. I want to think how Jesus thinks, because God's Spirit knows what is in God's mind, and that same Spirit dwells in us. Total wisdom, total knowledge, total understanding are available from God to us, and I want to tap into them.

After desire and expectation comes a specific burden for someone, somewhere, or something. When we expect God to use us to prophesy, we look around for the person whom God wants to touch. Before opening our mouth, we need to pray for that individual, asking God for His burden for them. Prophets must be concerned for that person: "Lord, please speak to her; and if I can help that process, I am willing." Nothing in the prophetic is scarier than having someone prophesy over you without feeling an ounce of concern or love for you.

It is burden that reveals God's heart. When we have a burden for something and we're praying, the Holy Spirit enables us to begin to put that into words. We start to feel that God wants to say and do something. This brings us into a sense of conviction, and it is conviction that produces expression. When we're convinced that God wants to say something, the desire, will, and means to express it all fall into place.

> **EXPECTATION IS: IT'S GOING TO RAIN; SELL YOUR UMBRELLA!**

The expression can vary. Sometimes, I may pick people out in a meeting setting and ask them to stand. Other times, God may get me to pick people out and I will ask them to come to the front of the room. At this point, I may not have received any prophetic words for them, but I have a sense of burden and expectation that God wants to do something. I call them out while asking God, "What do You want to do?" As I pray over the first person, the gift begins to flow, and God does something amazing.

We take that kind of risk because we expect God to move. We expect Him to show up. Therefore, when we go into places with expectation, there is a high probability that we will move in the prophetic gift. We need to anticipate what God wants to do and choose to work with Him to accomplish it.

God gives us a burden about things because He wants to speak and act. As far as He is concerned, a burden is a declaration to us that He wants to speak through us and use us in this situation. He has chosen us to work with Him because He has a burden for that particular person. This is a rare, and welcome, privilege for any of us.

Again, those steps are desire, expectation, burden, conviction, and expression. We can stir up the gift of prophecy by having the right motives. When we want to see a person blessed, healed, restored, and released, we are sharing the heart of God. We have put ourselves into the place where God can use us.

All of us can prophesy; the gift of prophecy is resident in each of us. We may not be called to be prophets, but every one of us can prophesy, and I hope we will seek that gift out more.

STARTING WHERE YOU ARE

Prophets need to allow God to push them into the revelatory. Sometimes, it is good to start at a low point. If we have had a difficult day, it is not wise to start with a massive prophetic word. We ought to start where our level of faith is and build from there.

GOD IS THE SAME IN AND OUT OF SEASON

Praying for people is a wonderful way to build our own sense of expectation. Once we start praying for someone, it is a short jump into the prophetic, because the two disciplines use the same faculties. When we ask God what we should pray, the Holy Spirit answers us. Suddenly, our spirits feel as though we should be praying something else, and we jump from prayer into the prophetic.

On days when our expectancy needs to be built up, we should not allow ourselves to be placed under incredible pressure. We should start small. If we feel low, start low: God doesn't mind, and He will build us up. In the twinkle of an eye, He can lead us into revelation.

We must start where we can. The last meeting we were in may have been a high point of revelation, but that doesn't mean we can come in at the same level every time. Sometimes we do, and sometimes we don't. A lot can happen between meetings. We need to allow God to push us into the supernatural.

I once met with thirty pastors in Germany and delivered an incredibly detailed, personal prophetic word to each of them. It was a high point of anointing: as soon as I finished with one, I picked up with another. The Lord was phenomenal that day — it had nothing to do with me.

The next morning, I was exhausted after a terrible night's sleep. Suddenly, I didn't have faith for anything anymore. So I started from scratch, just praying for people. I know that as long as I can pray, I can prophesy. My faith may be low, but it is never a problem for God.

We cannot maintain the high spots. There is a reason why Jesus led the disciples off the mountain after the Transfiguration. We can't live at that high level all the time. Our role is to be ourselves, and to be loved by God. As long as we are loved by Him, we can feel a burden for someone else.

We cannot operate from a continuous flow of the Spirit. For every flow there has to be an ebb in our experience.

What we do in the ebb is just as important as what we do in the flow. We learn lordship in the valley and the mountain. He is Lord of every life experience. Nothing prevents Him from being God. We must experience Him in the depths as well as the heights. We must learn to be a contribution when everything is against us.

When I prophesy out of my own low places of life, there is no diminishing of power. The Spirit is the same. The release of anointing and the impact of the Spirit may be different but no less real and full of truth. Humility comes to our aid at times like this. Be sure to keep your life on the altar. The Lord will set fire to the sacrifice we offer Him.

We don't always have to hear God in the moment, either. He can speak to us ahead of time about what we will face, who we will meet, and what we should do. Once, while preparing for a tour of America, God gave me almost two hundred prophetic words for people before leaving England. I wrote them all down in my journal—what people would be wearing, the color of their hair, their glasses, even where they would be sitting. He had messages for each of them.

At one point in the tour, I felt terrible. I hadn't slept well for a few nights and had come to a church that was bursting with expectancy. Of course, I felt like death warmed over. My faith, my confidence, my life: it was all on the floor. As all eyes turned to look at me, I just told God I could pray for one person, and hopefully that would build enough faith in me to pray for another. "What should I do, Lord?" I asked.

"Just read to them out of the book," He said. I opened up my journal and looked around the room. Sure enough, the first guy was there, wearing a dark blazer just like God had shown me. So I picked him out and prophesied. Over that conference, I think I did all of the people out of that book. God had provided for them and for me because He is relentlessly kind. He knew the warfare that would surround me on this particular tour and made arrangements beforehand to be with me in the pressure and to support my personal fragility. That's His nature.

HOW DOES PROPHECY COME?

All of us have a distinctive language with God and a unique way of how revelation comes to us. As we grow in the prophetic, we learn how our own gift manifests itself most often.

VISIONS. Sometimes, revelation comes through visions, pictures, or even moving scenes. Many of us have probably had a picture that has sparked something in us. Generally, there are two types of vision.

First, there is the *unremarkable vision* that uses everyday things around us, and maybe even uses our own understanding of things to speak prophetically. In Jeremiah 1:11–12, we witness this kind of vision: *"Moreover, the word of the Lord came to me, saying, 'Jeremiah, what do you see?' And I said, 'I see the branch of an almond tree.' Then the Lord said to me, 'You have seen well, for I am ready to perform My word.'"* When God asked the prophet what he saw, Jeremiah looked around and noticed the almond tree branch. It was a perfectly common and ordinary sight, totally unremarkable. However, the interpretation, timing, and specific need of the people combined to produce a positive and significant prophetic contribution.

There are times when we can use our own human knowledge with the picture we have been given. I was once in a meeting of several hundred people, about to speak, when the Lord directed me to a young woman in the middle aisle. I asked her to stand up, and as she did, God showed me a picture of a hazel tree. I knew the type of tree because my father and I had been landscape gardeners. All I had was this picture, so I asked the Lord, "What do You want to say?" There was nothing. I started in with what I knew: "I'm seeing a picture of a hazel tree," and began to describe its properties from what I could remember from my training.

"It's got beautiful flowers and fruit," I said. "It can grow almost anywhere, it's resistant to disease, and its bark and flowers can be used for medicinal purposes as a tonic or a sedative that brings comfort from pain. It's very hardy and resilient."

GOD'S SUPER COMPLEMENTS OUR NATURAL

As soon as I came to the end of that statement, I knew what God wanted to do. "That's how God sees you," I continued. "He thinks you're beautiful and that you're going to bear good fruit in your life. You mustn't be worried that you're no good; you're tough and able to resist the enemy. You'll grow in almost any situation." As I moved prophetically, she cried and her friends cheered and laughed.

I finished prophesying, prayed for her, and taught my seminar. At the end of the meeting, she came to me.

"Thanks for what you said. You don't know this, but my name is Hazel," she told me. Apparently, that same afternoon, she and her friends had been drinking tea, and Hazel had been in a bad mood. "Hazel. Stupid name, Hazel," she had said. "Why couldn't I have been called by a prettier name? I hate it, and I wish I could change it."

God, in His incredible sense of humor, had picked her out and given me a vision of a hazel tree. "Excuse Me," He was saying, "but I chose your name. I gave it to you, and I gave it to you for this purpose." She told me that she had cried because she realized that her name had been given to her for a reason. When she was in the womb, God had named her Hazel. What a powerful word from a perfectly ordinary and common source.

Second, a vision can be *supernatural*, rather than unremarkable. Acts 10 recounts the story of two men. One was a Greek who was devout, kind, trustworthy. God chose to reveal Himself to this man in a sovereign way. The other man was a Jew who was loud, impetuous, and racist. God wanted to put Cornelius and Peter together, but how? How could He unite them when they were separated by such a religious, national, and cultural divide—especially in the heart of one man who had been taught separatism from birth?

God chose to minister a supernatural vision to Peter in order to unlock what had become a form of national prejudice in his heart. He was given a vision of a sheet lowered from heaven, holding a full variety of edible species. A voice said, *"Arise, Peter, kill and eat."*

DO NOT LOOK TO THE PAST FOR SIGNS OF GOD WHEN HE IS DOING A NEW THING

Peter's first reaction was typical for his life: "I can't do that because these things are unholy, unclean, and I've never done that sort of thing in my life." God's voice boomed: *"What God has cleansed, you must not call common."* It happened three times, leaving Peter totally bewildered. What on earth did the vision mean? He had no interpretation for it, but while he was meditating on it, the Holy Spirit gave him some instructions.

"Behold, three men are seeking you," the Spirit said. *"Arise, therefore, go down with them, doubting nothing; for I have sent them."* Peter went with the men to Cornelius's house, preached the gospel, watched as the Holy Spirit fell on those men, and saw a completely new kind of church be born.

Sometimes we can get pictures that have a prophetic interpretation. Some are diagnostic in the sense that they give us information about things. Others may lead us into a word of knowledge, telling us something that has happened or is currently under way. When we receive a vision like that, our first step is to ask, "Father, in light of this, what is it You want to say?" Do not speak out the first thing you receive, because it may be diagnostic and could result in prophesying a problem, not an answer.

If we practice the art of waiting quietly, perhaps just for a few moments before we open our mouth to prophesy, we may glorify God more in the delivery and save ourselves some considerable heartache. Most mistakes in prophecy occur because we rush in with what we believe God is saying while He may still be speaking.

WHEN WE KNOW THE PURPOSE OF SOMETHING, WE CAN SEE THE POWER IN IT

We can also receive revelation through *moving pictures*, like a movie screen. We will see a portion of a scene, like the one I recounted earlier in this book of the adulterous husband, his redheaded secretary, and the Connaught Hotel. I saw them walk into the hotel together, check in, receive a room key, and get into the elevator. This was a moving picture.

THE PURPOSE OF VISIONS

It is not my intention to do more than give a thumbnail sketch at this moment regarding visions. In a later book in the series we shall look at the phenomenon of visions, dreams, dark sayings, and mysteries in greater detail. If you wish to follow up your understanding of visions, the following are some useful scriptures.

- To bring encouragement, to stir up hope regarding the promises of the Lord (see Genesis 15:1–6)
- To proclaim the calling of another (see Luke 1:22)
- The revelation of hidden things and interpreting of dreams (see Daniel 2:19)
- To bring good news (see Luke 24:23)
- For the sake of guiding people and instructing them on unfamiliar paths (see Acts 9:10)
- To change a cultural mindset (see Acts 10:9–16)
- To declare the will of God in mission (see Acts 16:9–10)

DREAMS. Some people receive revelation through dreams. I don't sleep much, and I don't seem to dream. In fact, I can remember only two dreams in my life, but they were both very significant.

Numbers 12:6 provides a biblical precedent for prophetic dreams: *"Then He said, 'Hear now My words: If there is a prophet among you, I, the LORD, make Myself known to him in a vision; I speak to him in a dream.'"* The Bible is full of examples of how God speaks in dreams. God spoke to Pharaoh in a dream only Joseph could interpret. The same thing happened with Nebuchadnezzar, and only Daniel could understand it. Joseph had a dream about Mary: the angel said, "Marry the girl!" That dream changed his mind because he was doubtful about the pregnancy before it (see Matthew 1). The so-called three wise men were warned in a dream to avoid King Herod. Later on, Joseph had another dream instructing him to take Mary and Jesus to Egypt. These were very practical, very prophetic dreams.

Dream interpretation is a gift produced by meditating on the dreams we have had and asking God for His take on them. *"Daniel had understanding in all visions and dreams,"* says Daniel 1:17. One of my closest friends has a gift of interpreting dreams. If you are a dreamer, you need to write down your dreams and work through them with God. Open them up for comment and prayer — they may be for you or for someone else. It may or may not be relevant, and a few weeks down the road, you may want to put it on the shelf. Get in the habit of writing things down; treat a dream as you would a prophecy.

THE PURPOSE OF DREAMS

These scripture references may be helpful in determining a deeper purpose for dreams than has been outlined here. A future book is planned to look at this in some detail. However, these are the scriptures to get you started on your journey of understanding dreams and interpretation.

- Proclamation regarding a future event or promise (see Genesis 28:12–15)

- To declare guidance and provide interpretation (see Genesis 31:10)

- Declare a purpose (see Genesis 31:24)

- To prepare us for the future, using foreknowledge of an event or circumstance (see Genesis 40:5)

- To provide warnings of future events (see Genesis 41:1–7)

- Releasing confirmation to encourage another. (see Judges 7:13–14)

- Future pronouncements (see Daniel 2)

- Future revelation (see Daniel 7)

- For encouragement in difficult circumstances (see Matthew 1:19–21)

- To expose the purpose of the enemy (see Matthew 1:19–21)

There are obviously more. The storyline around these instances will help to provide a framework for the context in which to understand each element.

SEEING WORDS. Revelation can also come by seeing one or two words over people. I have seen words such as "faith" and "healing" appear on someone's forehead. Those words alert us that God wants to say something and that He has marked a person's life with something He wants to reveal.

When we see a word, we can step back into our spirit and ask God what He wants to say. Into that quietness, God can drop a prophetic word. That first vital word activates our spirits; usually, it triggers a conceptual understanding of what the Holy Spirit wants to say. For example, seeing the word "healing" over someone can cause us to ask questions such as:

WE GROW BY ASKING QUESTIONS

- Is it healing for themselves?

SMITH WIGGLESWORTH

Lived: 1859 to 1947

Prophetic Synopsis: Few evangelists have pushed the kind of religious buttons Smith Wigglesworth pushed. His methods seem bizarre, but the fruit from his life and ministry was profound.

Wigglesworth's wife, Polly, was a powerful preacher, but Smith was painfully shy. He hated to speak in public, until the day the Holy Spirit got a hold of him. In 1907, he received the gift of tongues and was a changed man. As he preached that first Sunday, his wife was stunned: "That's not my Smith... What's happened to the man?" What had happened was a touch from God: "God once said to me, 'Wigglesworth, I'm going to burn you up till there's no Wigglesworth left; only Jesus will be seen.'"

His message was simple. "There are four principles we need to maintain: First, read the Word of God. Second, consume the Word of God until it consumes you. Third, believe the Word of God. Fourth, act on the Word of God." It was the way he acted on the Word of God that offended religious-spirited people. The stories of his healings are legendary.

There was the time he kicked a deformed baby across the stage. When the child landed, it was whole. Another time, a frail, crippled woman came up for prayer. Wigglesworth was impatient with her so he commanded her to walk. The woman stumbled around for a few moments, until the evangelist walked up behind her and pushed her. She fell forward into a run and Wigglesworth followed her up the aisle, shouting, "Run, woman, run!" She ran all right—right out of the building, but completely healed! On another occasion, Wigglesworth punched a man—wearing a hospital gown—who was suffering from cancer. When he got up, he was healed. "I don't hit people, I hit the devil. If they get in the way, I can't help it. You can't deal gently with the devil, nor comfort him; he likes comfort," he said

During his ministry, Smith Wigglesworth raised twenty-three people from the dead, including his own wife. He attributed his success to one person: God. "I know the Lord laid His hand on me. Filled! A flowing, quickening, moving flame of God."

Key Comment: "Only believe. Fear looks, faith jumps."

Sources: Stanley Burgess and Gary McGee, editors, *Dictionary of Pentecostal and Charismatic Movements* (Grand Rapids, MI: Zondervan, 1996). Roberts Liardon, *God's Generals* (Tulsa, OK: Albury Publishing, 1996).

- Is it healing for a family member or someone close to them?
- Does it indicate a healing gift will operate in their church?
- Is the Lord moving the individual into a healing gift?
- Is the Lord calling forth a full-on healing ministry?

As we ask the Lord questions in our spirits, the concept of where and how healing will be released will become clear. We can then aim the word in the right direction.

It is the same principle with less definitive words such as "peace." A prophet believes that the Holy Spirit wants to speak a genuine word of peace into the life of an individual. Where? How? Why? Peace into what area? What turmoil exists that needs peace to overcome it? Is it peace for financial worries, employment difficulties, relational problems, health issues, or something else? Where do we aim a word like that? To what area does the Lord wish to bring peace?

Our hearts must be on the same wavelength as God's, or we lose valuable perspective and power. The Bible teaches us that we have a High Priest, Jesus, who can be touched by the feeling of our infirmities. He is in tune with our feelings. In prophecy, we are seeking to communicate the spirit of the word, not just an abstract concept. A prophecy should impact a person's spirit, not just his or her mind.

Sometimes God uses a sentence or phrase that we picked up elsewhere and for some reason stays in our mind or memory. The Holy Spirit may use it as a catalyst when He wants to speak to someone. It could be something we read, heard on TV or the radio, and the Spirit brings it back to our remembrance.

One sentence I heard when praying for a woman was "Carry on doing on Earth what in heaven you are famous for." It obviously begs the question: "What is she famous for in heaven?" I saw a picture of her dancing in a living room setting. The Father showed me that she had danced as part of her devotional in worship but now that she was older had discontinued this form of private intimacy. The Lord wanted her to know that He loved it; she blessed Him by doing it and He wished for her to continue.

> **GOD LOVES BOTH THE REVEALED AND THE PROCEEDING WORD THAT HE SPEAKS!**

SCRIPTURE. The Bible can be an aid to prophecy. The Holy Spirit makes scripture come alive to us in a variety of ways: by personal messages, specific instruction, the revealing of God's essential nature, the process of truth and good teaching on the doctrines and tenets of spirituality and faith. He loves to prophetically inspire us also and will use the Bible to lift a curtain on an aspect of our future relationship and walk with God. He will use scripture to act as a catalyst for the prophetic word to present a particular message to someone. Often I have given prophecy from a passage of Scripture. Verses pop into our hearts and suddenly the prophetic spirit begins to move on it.

I prayed for a man once who worked within a very politically motivated group. People hated him because he was a Spirit-filled Christian. The knives were out; people were altering his work, hiding memos, and being obstructive in every possible way. They wanted him out and a friend of theirs in. The pressure on him was building, and he began to wonder if he was even supposed to be at his job.

As we prayed, God gave me Psalm 35. When I read it, I felt stirred up because it was all about fighting against the enemy, taking hold of the armor, believing that God is our salvation, having angels on our side, and turning those against us into confusion and dishonor. I put the Bible down and prophesied out of that psalm.

A short time later, several of his main antagonists were prosecuted for fraud, drug abuse, and mismanagement of funds. They were fired. Three Spirit-filled Christians took their place. That prophecy was a vital word to stand, fight, and see the salvation of God come.

IMPRESSIONS. God is at work in the small things as befits someone who absolutely has no ego, just a compelling sense of who He is and what He wants to be for His people. He loves the big picture but knows that the real power in something always lies in the attention to detail. He invites us into His world through the small things.

He never announces Himself. He tells you that He will come and invites you to wait for Him. Most of our inherent spirituality is waiting on the Lord. It is in learning how to attend on Him. This is not passive waiting only. We can wait on God on the busiest day. It is a subtle lifting of the heart in thanksgiving or worship. It is the beautiful habit of rejoicing, finding joy in the Father in everything. It is in the practice of God consciousness in our thinking, in allowing our heart to be filled with the wonder of Him, in living a simple life of astonishment at His continual goodness. It is in developing a certainty in the kindness of God. It is loving the laughter and cheeriness of the Holy Spirit. It is in being wrapped in the power of grace that is in the Lord Jesus, eyes filling with tears at the thought of His sacrifice. It is in cherishing the life, the freedom, and the dependency on His name and nature.

> **LOVE THE CHEERINESS OF THE HOLY SPIRIT!**

There are many ways to remain in abiding in the Lord. To dwell, stay, and remain in the place of love, favor, and expectation of His presence. Into this lifestyle the Father drops His still, small voice, caressing our hearts with a whisper. His touch is powerful yet so faint we could easily miss it if we are not practicing His presence.

An impression is a finger touch from God. It is an inkling, a notion, a tiny idea in the back of our mind or the forefront of our heart. It is a rabbit trail that leads to a goat track that becomes a pathway leading to a street, then a road that develops into a highway that becomes a freeway and the interstate right into His throne room.

God loves Jerusalem but chooses to begin something in a Bethlehem. He loves a huge palace but births something in a stable. He likes king-sized four-poster beds but loves to put something precious in a cow's feeding trough. He is easily overlooked.

When we contemplate hearing from God, we can think of angels as messenger spirits, prophets with all the drama that unfolds around them, signs as big as a billboard. We don't think of whispers, faint touches, notions and ideas that form in the quietness of our hearts. We don't understand the pleasure that God finds in whispering, the joy that He has in a slight caress of our heart.

When we practice the joy in waiting on Him, our hearts become attuned to the slightest possibility of His coming. He comes like a lion, not in roaring with power, but in stealth—a velvet whisper of sound so slight only your own stillness can detect it. One time in Africa I was in a hide at night with a hunting guide, waiting for a lion to show up at a kill. Armed with a night sight we waited through a cold African night. We had chained part of a fresh buffalo kill in the lower branches of a tree. For hours we waited. My eyelids grew heavy. Several times my friend nudged me back to wakefulness. I soaked my bandana in water, scrubbing my face, willing myself to stay awake. At the moment I was

IMPRESSIONS ENGAGE OUR HEARTS WITH THE LORD

convinced our vigil had been fruitless, my guide whispered in my ear, "He is here!"

I looked through my night sight binoculars and could see nothing. I knew my guide would not point him out to me; that was not our agreement. I wanted to seek the lion out for myself. I wanted to develop the patience in waiting, the stillness in being watchful. I looked carefully. Using each square foot as a grid, I tested everything, looking for something that looked right but did not belong. Listening is like that, isolating a certain sound from all the noises of life.

I saw the grass moving ever so slightly and realized it was in contradiction to the wind. I looked in the top part of the grass and eventually could see a shadow and then finally the tip of his ear as he settled down a few yards from the kill. He was testing the wind himself, looking for something that did not belong. I held my breath, willing my body into the comfort of stillness. We waited for what seemed like an hour or so but in reality was about twenty minutes. Suddenly he was there! In full view, huge, majestic, wild.

I drank in the sight of him. I gorged on his form, watching him eat. His strong teeth tore at the meat. The sounds of his eating filled the night. Then just as suddenly, he was gone. An empty chain and flattened grass was the only witnesses to his ever having been present.

The sounds of his coming and going were so slight that his visitation took on dream form.

So like God. Silent, present, still—to people who train themselves in quietness, worship, and peace. The Father loves stillness and quietness. The Holy Spirit is so patient and diligent to train us in peace and the art of tranquility, the calm joyfulness that waits with simplicity. He will come.

An impression in this context, is an arresting thought, that says, "Stop. Wait. Consider this!" It is a flag on the play of life that says stop, go back, you have missed something. It is an inner conviction that God is near, that He is brooding over our circumstances. We feel His peace before we hear His sound. It is a witness within that provokes us to wait. We tune in knowing He will speak. His voice can be strong or faint; that does not matter. The important thing is, we have tuned in through our inner quietness.

Impressions lead to experiences that may use our emotions. Sometimes I have looked at someone in the spirit and have had a sense of looking back whilst feeling pain or anguish. Silently I can breathe out my inner question to the Holy Spirit. "What happened in the past that was so traumatic for him?" Then I wait for the next piece, and the next, and the one after. Each piece of revelation the Holy Spirit releases can arrive in our heart with a progressively stronger sound carrying with it a powerful conviction not only about the diagnosis but also about the intentionality of what the Father has for this individual—now!

Moments of release and power can be so huge that they are out of all proportion to the initial reception, the first whisper.

Sometimes too, the initial contact and the final release are both slight, faint, and seemingly innocuous. There seems to be no impact on the individual we minister to in prophecy. We may as well have just read out a shopping list over them. There is no visible reaction or response, just…nothing.

(The temptation here is to go further in prophecy than you should just to get a response. Now you are prophesying for yourself, for your own reputation, so that others present can see your anointing).

People respond differently to prophecy. Whilst some respond verbally and visibly, others may do a passable imitation of a brick wall!

Some people show you nothing; it does not mean that nothing has happened. Several days later we discover that the impact was absolutely enormous! Alternatively we find out later that everything is amazingly different but there was no evidence of power and breakthrough. It was all like a silent movie but unmistakably the hand of God. He seldom works as we would wish. I have learned just to ask for His presence, never to dictate how He should come.

Sometimes I have felt myself looking forward and feeling joy or peace. I realize that the Lord is about to release something in the gap between where a person is currently and the person that is emerging next in their relationship with the Father.

The Lord uses impressions relationally. It is one of His ways to engage our hearts in conversation and dialogue. We ask questions so that we may explore His heart for this person. It is in what we feel that God is feeling for this individual that the real power of prophecy is earthed. God uses our hearts to indicate the passion of His intentionality. Every human being has three major needs: to be loved, to belong, and to be significant.

IMPRESSIONS CONNECT WITH OUR EMOTIONS

Prophecy becomes an impartation when we feel what God is feeling for someone. The strength of His intentionality as seen in Jeremiah 29:11 becomes the driving force behind the prophecy we release.

> *"For I know the plans that I have for you," declares the LORD, "plans for welfare and not for calamity to give you a future and a hope. Then you will call upon Me and come and pray to Me, and I will listen to you. You will seek Me and find Me when you search*

for Me with all your heart. I will be found by you," declares the LORD, "and I will restore your fortunes and will gather you from all the nations and from all the places where I have driven you," declares the LORD, "and I will bring you back to the place from where I sent you into exile."

The goodness of God initiates something wonderful in our hearts. His intentionality is thrilling! When we connect with it, our hearts soar and we are compelled to call on His name. Intentionality breeds faith. We are designed by the Creator to respond to His advances. It is in our DNA. It is part of our Christlike nature that the Holy Spirit is developing in us. When we feel the weight of the Father's intention, we want to be intentional too! As He is, so are we in this world.

His intentions toward us are incredible. His delight and desire for us set us free to pursue Him. We all want to be with people who want to be with us. We joyfully go where we are celebrated. God's intentionality forms a desire in me to call on Him, to come, pray, and listen to Him because I know that I am so welcome!

THE LORD ORIGINATES EVERYTHING!

My capacity to become wholehearted is never generated from my own efforts. We receive from the Lord what He most wants us to become!

Or WHO HAS FIRST GIVEN TO HIM THAT IT MIGHT BE PAID BACK TO HIM AGAIN? For from Him and through Him and to Him are all things. To Him be the glory forever. Amen. (Romans 11:35–36)

Every good thing given and every perfect gift is from above, coming down from the Father of lights, with whom there is no variation or shifting shadow. (James 1:17)

John answered and said, "A man can receive nothing unless it has been given him from heaven. (John 3:27)

Yet for us there is but one God, the Father, from whom are all things and we exist for Him; and one Lord, Jesus Christ, by whom are all things, and we exist through Him. (1 Corinthians 8:6)

For as the woman originates from the man, so also the man has his birth through the woman; and all things originate from God. (1 Corinthians 11:12)

For by Him all things were created, both in the heavens and on earth, visible and invisible, whether thrones or dominions or rulers or authorities—all things have been created through Him and for Him. He is before all things, and in Him all things hold together. (Colossians 1:16–17)

*For it was fitting for Him, for whom are all things, and through whom are all things, in bringing many sons to glory, to perfect the author of their salvation through sufferings. (Hebrews 2:10)
No longer do I call you slaves, for the slave does not know what his master is doing; but I have called you friends, for all things that I have heard from My Father I have made known to you.* (John 15:15)

In this is love, not that we loved God, but that He loved us and sent His Son to be the propitiation for our sins. We love, because He first loved us. (1 John 4:10, 19)

Everything originates in God! We are His beloved. Only God can love God. It takes God to love God. The love of God comes to our hearts as part of a great cycle of intentionality. We receive His love; it touches, affects, influences, and changes us. Then we give back to the Lord the very love that He gave us in the first place.

We are empowered by the Holy Spirit to fulfill the first commandment simply because the Father Himself lives by the very same principles! We love Him because He first loved us. Everything comes down to us as a gift and we then give it back to God. In creation God uses the action of rainfall soaking the earth and then returning to heaven as the process of evaporation where clouds are replenished. Everything with God is cyclical, including the times and seasons.

Prophecy fits in with this cycle. It announces what the Lord will do and reveals our part in the process. Impressions are about asking questions and relating to the Holy Spirit in the moment.

Never launch out on an impression. Instead, take it before God and allow the larger process to unfold in more revelation. If we move out too quickly, we release blessing in measure rather than fullness. It is when we ask questions that the rabbit trail becomes a bigger pathway leading to a more powerful encounter.

The Holy Spirit is teaching us how to relax in God's intentionality, then how to respond to His advances. In prophecy we make people aware of God's intention and then enable them to receive and respond. Impressions are primarily for the giver, not the receiver of prophecy.

They bring us into a relationship with the Father that releases His heart, passion, and total intention. We are moved by His nature. We are impacted ourselves and we seek to move out of what we are discovering of the goodness of God in the face of Jesus Christ.

BEING QUIET IS KEY

In 1 Kings 19:11–12, we read an interesting story of God interacting with his prophet Elijah:

Then He said, "Go out, and stand on the mountain before the LORD." And behold, the LORD passed by, and a great and strong wind tore into the mountains and broke the rocks in pieces before the LORD, but the LORD was not in the wind; and after the wind an earthquake, but the LORD was not in the earthquake; and after the earthquake, a fire, but the LORD was not in the fire; and after the fire a still, small voice.

The voice of the Lord is like a whisper at times; it can be so soft that we strain to hear it. That's why being still and quiet is so important to prophecy. In the peace of God, revelation flows. There have been times when I have been so at rest that I've heard the whisper of God, turned to a person near me, and said, "Can you hear that?" It's like He spoke out loud. If we have stillness on the inside, even the whisper of God sounds loud to us.

Too many Christians have no idea about the quietness of God. I remember working with some men in America for the first time. We were at a conference together, and I was just getting to know them.

They were nice guys, and we sat in a hotel restaurant, talking and laughing. It was an ordinary, lighthearted conversation. After a while, they looked at me and said they had a word for me.

They laid their hands on me and yelled at me in perfect King James English. They almost rubbed my head bald. They pushed me all over the place, shouting so loudly they were spitting in my face. They were sending me to some country, somewhere, in their prophecy. It was awful.

"What are you doing?" I asked, stopping them in mid-sentence.

"What do you mean?" they said.

"What are you doing?" I repeated.

"We're prophesying over you," they said.

> **WHEN WE RELAX INTO GOD'S INTENTIONALITY, WE CAN RESPOND TO HIS ADVANCES**

"I know that," I replied, "but I don't understand the funny language. Why were we having a conversation on one level and then we start praying and you speak in old King James English? Why are you trying to give me a migraine? And I had a shower this morning; why are you spitting all over me? I'm not deaf, but you're shouting at me. Please, I'm not trying to be rude or anything. I'm always ready to learn, but I just don't understand this. Why do you have one way of speaking in life and another in ministry?

They couldn't think of a reason why. I kept going: "Okay, why put my head in a vice? Is there a reason? Because that was pretty painful. I have indentations on my skull." Again, they had no reason behind their actions.

"Why has your voice level gone up fifty decibels?" I continued. "It's unhygienic to spit on someone. I really appreciate your ministry but maybe you could change your approach. This one has left me really struggling and I can't understand a word you're saying."

I would have loved to have seen those three men come to my church in Southampton, UK, where I was living at the time. The place would have been rolling in laughter at the rudeness of their methods. My friends and church family would have howled.

After the prophecy, we had a conversation about it. I think we always need to demystify the prophetic. One of the problems with revelatory people is that they try to elevate it to an almost mystical connection with God. But God is sometimes so ordinary in His approach that we miss His voice.

Samuel almost missed God's voice in 1 Samuel 3. He heard the voice of God and thought it was Eli. Three times he heard the voice of God, and three times he thought it was Eli. Finally, Eli understood what was going on. *"Go lie down,"* he told the boy in 1 Samuel 3:9, *"and it shall be, if He calls you, that you must say, 'Speak, LORD, for Your servant hears.'"*

God's voice is ordinary and non-religious. There is nothing spooky about it. When we are speaking prophetically, we should invest our words with the heart of God. Our language should be normal and understandable, and as common with our usual style of conversation as possible.

FATHER LIKES TO COME THROUGH THE ORDINARY

A large percentage of prophecy is stating the obvious. God loves us; He cares for us. We shouldn't apologize if the word we have doesn't feel fresh or exotic. Prophecy can be like an old scripture you've read a thousand times — you become used to it until God reinvigorates and brings it to your attention in a new way. When we look at a word and dismiss it as boring or usual, we look at prophecy the wrong way. God wants every person to feel His love, and He will reveal to us the way to communicate that seemingly well-worn theme. People need to hear the obvious sometimes. God has a way of putting fresh emphasis on things they already know.

A prophet is always being tested in ministry. Walk softly in the prophetic before God. If you're not sure of something, stay quiet. In the context of local church, most prophecy can wait a day, if not a week. Take time to pray about it because you can always come back to it. Prophesy at the level of faith you have. It is better to stop in prophecy than to go too far. It is always easier to add than to retract.

RHYTHM OF LIFE WITH GOD

One of the wonderful things about life with God is the rhythm we develop with Him. In creation, there is a rhythm. Night follows day. The seasons change. Birds migrate and return. The tide comes in and goes out. God's rhythmic imprint has been placed upon the earth and heavens. Our senses are aware of the rhythm of the world around us—we can smell the air and know what the weather will be like. We're used to the rhythm of the climate.

With God, we are always responding to something He is doing. Early in the day, we can be drawn into what God is doing. We're like children. What's Mom up to? Baking? Great, we'll help. Likewise, our Father works and we work. We love God because He first loved us. It is all about the rhythm of His Spirit.

The Holy Spirit will apply pressure to move us into the love of God. Like the moon draws the tide, He draws us to the love of God. Things may get worse as He tries to bring us into His rest, but we can trust that it is part of the rhythm of life with God.

God always makes the first move, and we return the favor. His delight is to love us, and our desire is to love Him. When we understand, and live in, the rhythm of God, we come into ministry in a much safer way. I can't say anything unless God speaks first. There is no pressure on me; it's all up to Him. When God says something, and faith fills my heart, then I can prophesy.

Most days, I am not consumed about the ministry. It is not a high priority when I could be in the presence of God. But isn't that what true ministry should be? Ministry, especially the prophetic, is about relating to God and doing, today, what He wants you to do. It is about matching the rhythm of His life. When we love who He is, minister to Him, and flow in His presence, we can be confident that God will use us as He sees fit.

GIVE WHAT YOU HAVE

If we practice the presence of God, then we never have to question the source of what we are hearing. Availability is one of the prime motivators of confidence. Because I wait on God, my availability connects with His intentionality. I can stir up the gift that is within me (see 2 Timothy 1:6) because I know that the Father loves to connect with people. I may not always have a prophecy, but I will have advice, wisdom, and a prayer to offer.

Everyone giving as they themselves are enabled is a key principle that covers all of life, not just spiritual gifts.

Every man shall give as he is able, according to the blessing of the LORD your God which He has given you. (Deuteronomy 16:17)

For if the readiness is present, it is acceptable according to what a person has, not according to what he does not have. (2 Corinthians 8:12)

But Peter said, "I do not possess silver and gold, but what I do have I give to you: In the name of Jesus Christ the Nazarene—walk!" (Acts 3:6)

We first give our will over to God. He works in us both to will and to do (see Philippians 2:12-13)!

The burden of the Lord is light and our partnership with Him is easy (see Matthew 11:28–30). We prophesy from a place of rest, humility, and peace. We give cheerfully because the Father is delighted with joy and rejoicing (see 2 Corinthians 9:7). The Father is always attracted to His own nature in us. He loves love, peace, joy, patience, and all the attributes of the Holy Spirit.

THE SPIRIT QUICKENS THE EVERYDAY THINGS

When our heart is open to His nature, even our ordinary words can be quickened by the Holy Spirit. Someone once described the supernatural as God's super on our natural. He loves to move through us. When we first begin to move in prophecy, of course there is mixture. There is always mixture! It is more obvious when we are just getting started and more subtle when we have been on the journey for a long time. Teachers and preachers have mixture. Pastors and counselors have mixture in their advice. Intercessors have mixture in their perceptions and prayers.

The Holy Spirit is so capable of sorting these things out. We have no need of suspicion or mistrust. We trust the Holy Spirit to witness to the God part and be kind about the other. *"We know in part and we prophesy in part"* (1 Corinthians 13:9).

False prophecy is not about getting it wrong. That is poor prophecy that arises out of our inexperience and lack of wisdom. False prophecy involves a deliberate and calculated attempt to lead people astray, usually for some selfish purpose: monetary gain, increasing a power base, sexual dominance. Sadly, in all walks of life and ministry there are people who are not saved below the waistline, have a big ego above the neck line, and the only balance they are about is the one in their local bank account!

TONGUES AND INTERPRETATION

Tongues is the language of men and angels (see 1 Corinthians 13:1). On the day of Pentecost many people heard messages in their own languages that men who had previously been fishermen could not possibly have learned. These were the same men who had been arrested by the priests and the Sadducees (see Acts 4). They were found to be ignorant and unlearned (see 4:13) but had obviously spent time with Jesus.

On many occasions I have spoken out publicly and in a tongue that I had not learned. The interpretation was given by people in the congregation and conference, who had heard their own language coming out of my mouth. One man in South Africa heard me say in his language

TONGUES IS THE LANGUAGE OF HEAVEN SPOKEN ON EARTH

(Nigerian) that his mother was praying for him to come to Christ. Which he did in that meeting! In Kentucky, USA, I spoke in flawless Cherokee for several minutes and reiterated a prophecy about a man and his family coming into a season of blessing and prosperity. The man who interpreted the tongue had been given that same word several weeks before by his brother's wife. He had not believed her, so she told him to write it down and pray for confirmation. I guess he got that!

> *Pursue love, yet desire earnestly spiritual gifts, but especially that you may prophesy. For one who speaks in a tongue does not speak to men but to God; for no one understands, but in his spirit he speaks mysteries. But one who prophesies speaks to men for edification and exhortation and consolation. One who speaks in a tongue edifies himself; but one who prophesies edifies the church. Now I wish that you all spoke in tongues, but even more that you would prophesy; and greater is one who prophesies than one who speaks in tongues, unless he interprets, so that the church may receive edifying.*
>
> *But now, brethren, if I come to you speaking in tongues, what will I profit you unless I speak to you either by way of revelation or of knowledge or of prophecy or of teaching? Yet even lifeless things, either flute or harp, in producing a sound, if they do not produce a distinction in the tones, how will it be known what is played on the flute or on the harp? For if the bugle produces an indistinct sound, who will prepare himself for battle? So also you, unless you utter by the tongue speech that is clear, how will it be known what is spoken? For you will be speaking into the air. There are,*

perhaps, a great many kinds of languages in the world, and no kind is without meaning.

If then I do not know the meaning of the language, I will be to the one who speaks a barbarian, and the one who speaks will be a barbarian to me. So also you, since you are zealous of spiritual gifts, seek to abound for the edification of the church. Therefore let one who speaks in a tongue pray that he may interpret. For if I pray in a tongue, my spirit prays, but my mind is unfruitful. What is the outcome then? I will pray with the spirit and I will pray with the mind also; I will sing with the spirit and I will sing with the mind also.

Otherwise if you bless in the spirit only, how will the one who fills the place of the ungifted say the "Amen" at your giving of thanks, since he does not know what you are saying? For you are giving thanks well enough, but the other person is not edified. I thank God, I speak in tongues more than you all; however, in the church I desire to speak five words with my mind so that I may instruct others also, rather than ten thousand words in a tongue. Brethren, do not be children in your thinking, yet in evil be infants, but in your thinking be mature.

In the Law it is written, "BY MEN OF STRANGE TONGUES AND BY THE LIPS OF STRANGERS I WILL SPEAK TO THIS PEOPLE, AND EVEN SO THEY WILL NOT LISTEN TO ME," says the Lord. So then tongues are for a sign, not to those who believe but to unbelievers; but prophecy is for a sign, not to unbelievers but to those who believe. Therefore if the whole church assembles together and all speak in tongues, and ungifted men or unbelievers enter, will they not say that you are mad?

But if all prophesy, and an unbeliever or an ungifted man enters, he is convicted by all, he is called to account by all; the secrets of his heart are disclosed; and so he will fall on his face and worship God, declaring that God is certainly among you. What is the outcome then, brethren? When you assemble, each one has a psalm, has a teaching, has a revelation, has a tongue, has an interpretation. Let all things be done for edification. If anyone speaks in a tongue, it should be by two or at the most three, and each in turn, and one must interpret; but if there is no interpreter, he must keep silent in the church; and let him speak to himself and to God. (1 Corinthians 14:1–28)

With all prayer and petition pray at all times in the Spirit, and with this in view, be on the alert with all perseverance and petition for all the saints. (Ephesians 6:18)

But you, beloved, building yourselves up on your most holy faith, praying in the Holy Spirit. (Jude 1:20)

These signs will accompany those who have believed: in My name they will cast out demons, they will speak with new tongues. (Mark 16:17)

Gathering them together, He commanded them not to leave Jerusalem, but to wait for what the Father had promised, "Which," He said, "you heard of from Me; for John baptized with water, but you will be baptized with the Holy Spirit not many days from now." So when they had come together, they were asking Him, saying, "Lord, is it at this time You are restoring the kingdom to Israel?" He said to them, "It is not for you to know times or epochs which the Father has fixed by His own authority; but you will receive power when the Holy Spirit has come upon you; and you shall be My witnesses both in Jerusalem, and in all Judea and Samaria, and even to the remotest part of the earth."

And after He had said these things, He was lifted up while they were looking on, and a cloud received Him out of their sight. And as they were gazing intently into the sky while He was going, behold, two men in white clothing stood beside them. They also said, "Men of Galilee, why do you stand looking into the sky? This Jesus, who has been taken up from you into heaven, will come in just the same way as you have watched Him go into heaven." Then they returned to Jerusalem from the mount called Olivet, which is near Jerusalem, a Sabbath day's journey away. When they had entered the city, they went up to the upper room where they were staying; that is, Peter and John and James and Andrew, Philip and Thomas, Bartholomew and Matthew, James the son of Alphaeus, and Simon the Zealot, and Judas the son of James. (Acts 1:4–13) For they were hearing them speaking with tongues and exalting God. (Acts 10:46)

And when Paul had laid his hands upon them, the Holy Spirit came on them, and they began speaking with tongues and prophesying. (Acts 19:6)

…and to another the effecting of miracles, and to another prophecy, and to another the distinguishing of spirits, to another various kinds of tongues, and to another the interpretation of tongues. And God has appointed in the church, first apostles, second prophets, third teachers, then miracles, then gifts of healings, helps, administrations, various kinds of tongues. All do not have gifts of healings, do they? All do not speak with tongues, do they? All do not interpret, do they? (1 Corinthians 12:10, 28, 30)

If I speak with the tongues of men and of angels, but do not have love, I have become a noisy gong or a clanging cymbal. (1 Corinthians 13:1).

Tongues is the language of heaven. It is the language of angels and the conversation of the Spirit. He loves to speak to us in our own language. Even more He loves to communicate to us and through us in a heavenly language that we can speak back to Him in prayer and in worship.

Tongues is the language of the secret place. It is the speech of intimacy. It is a lovers language. It is a warfare language also whereby we may speak out things in intercession that the enemy cannot understand. When we speak in tongues in this way, we communicate directly to heaven, which frustrates the spiritual opposition we face on certain days. The enemy loves to mess

> **THE LANGUAGE OF THE SECRET PLACE IS THE COMMUNICATION OF GOD'S HEART TO YOURS!**

with our mind, particularly when it comes to knowing what to pray. It is therefore particularly galling for him when I speak in tongues from my spirit, bypassing my own mind in the process. It is the secret language of heaven that originates in my spirit, not my head. I am in direct contact with heaven, so my faith rises as I pray this way. I encounter the Lord when I use my spirit language. The most amazing truth also is that I can ask for and receive an interpretation so that I may discover what I just prayed! A lot of my current crafted prayers have developed out of my secret language.

This is probably the chief reason why the enemy stirs up controversy about the gift of tongues. He hates it when the church prays in the will of God. He loathes secret languages that render him powerless to intervene. He is angry when we communicate directly with heaven over his head. He seeks control of our faith in order to sow unbelief, leading to demoralization and prayerlessness. He welcomes prayer that begins in doubt and questioning. He does not want believers to pray with God but toward Him. When we pray in the Spirit, we are asking God to do what He most wants to do. Praying in tongues gives me incredible confidence because the presence of God is in the language of heaven.

If there is any way that the enemy can stir up fear or misunderstanding about this amazing gift, then he will gladly take it. He tries to make out that this gift is really just a subjective emotional experience that overwhelms peoples senses, controls their will, and makes them vulnerable in their thinking. He does not want people understanding that tongues is an actual language that we can use in the same way as our native tongue.

We use different tones, intonations, decibels, inflections, and emotions in the same way we would our natural language. As with our usual language, we have to choose to speak it out. Our will is the vehicle for all our experiences with the Lord. *"He works in us to will and to do, for His own good pleasure"* (Philippians 2:13).

When we speak in tongues, our will is the vehicle that enables us to communicate in a language that puts us in direct connection with the heart of the Father. This is why Paul was thankful that he spoke in tongues more than anyone (see 1 Corinthians 14:18)! There is a strong link between the use of our heavenly language and our capacity to receive revelation.

Our flesh cannot move against us when we pray in the Spirit. Our mind can join the party but not spoil it. Interpretation makes our mind fruitful after the fact, not before.

All languages must grow. What is true in the natural is true in the Spirit. Vocabulary must develop. Our communication must take on a more adult form. It is sad in the Spirit to hear someone using the same few words that they have always used when they could have developed their heavenly language as they did their earthly one.

ALL LANGUAGE GROWS INTO A GREATER EXPRESSION OF CREATIVITY

When we first begin to communicate in this language to the Lord we receive key words and phrases just as we do in our usual language. Our supernatural language follows the same precedents as our natural one.

Language forms around syllables coming together. Words form as we speak and sentences unfold in the normal way. The difference is that the supernatural language arrives without our pre-thinking it. The Holy Spirit stirs us to speak but allows us to control the flow, intonation, inflection, and decibel level. We speak out of our heart where Christ lives. As with any language we must practice it continuously to become fluent.

I have spoken in tongues for more than thirty years (since 1972) and have now developed four heavenly languages with the help of the Holy Spirit. One is for my deepest moments of intimate worship, a love language that fills my heart with adoration of Jesus. I am surrounded by His presence, filled with His peace, and brimming over with His confidence. It's impossible not to smile with this language. The quiet joy of His presence radiates His pleasure and I am undone by love.

Another tongue I have developed with the Holy Spirit is for warfare situations. I choose to fight. I want to live in the territory where the clash of two kingdoms is most pronounced. This particular language puts an edge on my faith as a sharpening stone would on a sword blade. It stirs me up to fight. It refreshes me so that I am not weary. We beat the enemy by staying fresh. I love warfare. I want to relish the fight. I want to be a New Testament version of one of David's mighty men (see 2 Samuel 23:8–39). This language makes me stand up on the inside. My inner man of the spirit comes to attention and readiness. This particular language of the spirit increases my faith and energizes my relationship with the Lord. I see His majesty. I am filled with a sense of His sovereignty. It leads me into high praise and laughter—lots of laughter. It is our joy to be confident in the Lord.

A third language I have really helps me with my lifestyle of meditation and contemplation of God. I love to open my Bible and lay my hands on a particular passage and pray for some time in this contemplative prayer language. I am praying always for a spirit of wisdom and revelation to communicate with me in the knowledge of Christ (see Ephesians 1:16–18). I adore loving God with my mind as well as my heart. Thinking deeply about God is a huge pleasure in my life.

This particular language is so wonderful in enabling me to focus on the spirit of truth.

I love the Holy Spirit, His calmness and tranquility. I love His energy and incredible cheeriness. He makes me smile, giggle, and laugh out loud. I love His place in my heart. He is such a genius at everything and so amazingly happy. He is an astonishing tutor who loves to proclaim Jesus.

My fourth language is my everyday conversational communication with the Holy Spirit. It's the one I use to ask questions, stay in divine connection, query what is happening, prepare my heart for various events, and to generally acknowledge the Father in my heart. I love to pray in English the prayers that the Father has placed in my heart. This is praying with God rather than merely to God. These prayers originate in my prayer languages. The Holy Spirit interprets them to my mind from my heart.

EXPLICIT LANGUAGES FOR A SPECIFIC PURPOSE

When I sense that an interpretation is coming, I take a pen and paper and sit quietly. Words begin to form in my mind and I write them down. At times I may write key words and key phrases and then meditate on them for a while. Sentences begin to form, meaning opens up, and the knowledge of what to ask for fills my heart with confidence. I am praying with the answer, not to find one.

Other times I can write down the whole prayer verbatim. I cannot describe the joy of holding the answer to prayer in my hand before I have even prayed for it!

A prayer language is the language of prayer as God speaks it. Jesus ever lives to make intercession (see Hebrews 7:25) and the Spirit Himself intercedes for us with groanings too deep for words (see Romans

8:26). Wouldn't you want to know what they are praying? Having a supernatural prayer language is a phenomenal asset. Being able to interpret that language so that we can pray with the Spirit and with understanding pushes our prayer life into a place of power and pleasure. Is it any wonder that the enemy puts such controversy around these particular gifts? He is quite frantic to deny every believer access to such incredible grace and power. He has a vested interest in our powerlessness in prayer. The cessationist doctrine about the Holy Spirit and the gifts not being for the modern-day church has been one of his most memorable and powerful ongoing victories over the church. It has rendered the church impotent in the supernatural and has enabled the New Age movement to flourish uncontested by the body of Christ at large.

> **THERE IS NO PLACE IN OUR VOCABULARY OR LIFESTYLE FOR IMPOTENCE!**

These days are changing however. The church is gradually returning to her supernatural roots. Churches that were once anti-charismatic have moved toward the Holy Spirit in recent years, becoming non-charismatic (a huge change) and many are now quietly charismatic. In a post-modern world, the view of truth is very different. Everyone loves truth and seeks it, not necessarily in Christ. People appreciate my truth in Christ and want me to value their truth no matter where it is founded or rooted. The organ for receptivity of truth is no longer the ear. People used to come to church to hear the truth expressed in good preaching and teaching.

In a post-modern world, the organ for receptivity of truth is the eye. People want to see something. We live in a show and tell world. This is the perfect scenario for a church that loves to pray for the sick and believes in miracles. Signs and wonders are the currency of heaven.

They are the keys of the kingdom that unlock every religion and philosophy known to man. Prophecy, tongues, and interpretation allow us to gain specific access to people's hearts so that they hear what God knows about them. The secrets of their hearts are revealed (see 1 Corinthians 14:26). God knows the innermost dreams of every person. When a man or woman hears a person speaking in a tongue that is either a heavenly language or the language of the listener and their own dreams are being spoken, then worship is the result. People come to faith and certainty quickly when the church moves as heaven would. On Earth as it is in heaven is still the goal of God—to create an earth with the same environment and conditions that heaven regularly enjoys!

GOD HAS A LANGUAGE FOR YOU THAT INTERFERES WITH THE ENEMY

Anything less than that is a sub-standard gospel. Tongues and interpretation are a part of our empowering in the gospel. They are great tools for evangelism and people development. Prophecy is a great tool for discipleship and growing people. The word of knowledge and the word of wisdom allow the church to partake of the tremendous insights of heaven to a hurting and needy world.

On a flight to Hong Kong, as we were boarding in London, the Lord gave me a word of knowledge for the person next to me. This Chinese lady had lost several relatives in plane crashes and was paranoid about flying herself. I introduced myself, told her I was a Christian, relayed to her what the Lord had showed me, and expressed confidently that the Father would heal her of her fear of flying. She was shocked and intrigued but readily agreed to receive prayer. She ate, slept, read, and we talked during the long flight. Absolutely no fear! She accepted Christ. She had too much evidence not to!

Tongues and interpretation aid our communication both to God personally and of God to others. They are great gifts for building people up in the Lord. We can pray and sing in tongues, enabling our channel of communication in worship and intercession to remain open and functioning at a high level. They are a sign to unbelievers that God can know, understand, and communicate at the right level with them. They are faith builders that enable us to establish our relationship with the Lord at a deeper level more continuously. They strengthen and confirm us in Christ. They allow us greater freedom and intimacy in our fellowship with the Holy Spirit. They seriously interfere with the plans and purposes of the enemy because we are no longer subject to his mind games. In fact we can play a few games of our own!

> **THE NATURAL AND THE SPIRITUAL ALWAYS COMBINE IN THE FATHER'S HEART**

GOD USES EVERYDAY OBJECTS

The Father loves symbolism. Scripture is full of pictorial language, parables, allegories, and creative speech. God can and does communicate through physical objects.

> *The word which came to Jeremiah from the LORD saying, "Arise and go down to the potter's house, and there I will announce My words to you." Then I went down to the potter's house, and there he was, making something on the wheel. But the vessel that he was making of clay was spoiled in the hand of the potter; so he remade it into another vessel, as it pleased the potter to make. Then the word of the LORD came to me saying, "Can I not, O house*

of Israel, deal with you as this potter does?" declares the LORD. "Behold, like the clay in the potter's hand, so are you in My hand, O house of Israel." (Jeremiah 18:1–6)

God sent the prophet to the potter's house to both watch in the natural and hear in the Spirit. The Father uses the natural elements to speak prophetically in a symbolic manner. The Holy Spirit always interprets the will of the Father. The Lord loves to vary His methods of communication with us to teach us to be open to all forms and practices of divine connection.

Then the LORD said to me, "Even though Moses and Samuel were to stand before Me, My heart would not be with this people; send them away from My presence and let them go! And it shall be that when they say to you, 'Where should we go?' then you are to tell them, 'Thus says the LORD: "Those destined for death, to death; And those destined for the sword, to the sword; And those destined for famine, to famine; And those destined for captivity, to captivity."'

"I will appoint over them four kinds of doom," declares the LORD: "the sword to slay, the dogs to drag off, and the birds of the sky and the beasts of the earth to devour and destroy. I will make them an object of horror among all the kingdoms of the earth because of Manasseh, the son of Hezekiah, the king of Judah, for what he did in Jerusalem.

> "Indeed, who will have pity on you, O Jerusalem, Or who will mourn for you, Or who will turn aside to ask about your welfare? You who have forsaken Me," declares the LORD, "You keep going backward. So I will stretch out My hand against you and destroy you; I am tired of relenting!

> "I will winnow them with a winnowing fork at the gates of the land; I will bereave them of children, I will destroy My people; They did not repent of their ways. Their widows will be more numerous before Me than the sand of the seas; I will bring against them, against the mother of a young man, a destroyer at noonday; I will suddenly bring down on her anguish and dismay.

THE CREATOR WILL ALWAYS BE CREATIVE IN HOW HE COMMUNICATES

> "She who bore seven sons pines away; Her breathing is labored Her sun has set while it was yet day; She has been shamed and humiliated. So I will give over their survivors to the sword before their enemies," declares the LORD.

> Woe to me, my mother, that you have borne me as a man of strife and a man of contention to all the land! I have not lent, nor have men lent money to me, yet everyone curses me.

> The LORD said, "Surely I will set you free for purposes of good; Surely I will cause the enemy to make supplication to you in a time of disaster and a time of distress.

"Can anyone smash iron, iron from the north, or bronze?

"Your wealth and your treasures I will give for booty without cost, even for all your sins and within all your borders. Then I will cause your enemies to bring it into a land you do not know; for a fire has been kindled in My anger, It will burn upon you."

You who know, O LORD, remember me, take notice of me, and take vengeance for me on my persecutors. Do not, in view of Your patience, take me away; know that for Your sake I endure reproach. Your words were found and I ate them, and Your words became for me a joy and the delight of my heart; for I have been called by Your name, O LORD God of hosts.

I did not sit in the circle of merrymakers, nor did I exult. Because of Your hand upon me I sat alone, for You filled me with indignation.

Why has my pain been perpetual and my wound incurable, refusing to be healed? Will You indeed be to me like a deceptive stream with water that is unreliable?

Therefore, thus says the LORD, "If you return, then I will restore you—before Me you will stand; and if you extract the precious from the worthless, you will become My spokesman. They for their part may turn to you, but as for you, you must not turn to them.

> *"Then I will make you to this people a fortified wall of bronze; and though they fight against you, they will not prevail over you; for I am with you to save you and deliver you," declares the LORD.*
>
> *"So I will deliver you from the hand of the wicked, and I will redeem you from the grasp of the violent."* (Jeremiah 15)

Jeremiah receives specific instruction that combines physical objects with symbolic acts that are imbued with prophetic significance and spiritual meaning: Buy a clay jar first; take the key people of the day on a walk to a particular place and prophesy to them. Then Jeremiah has to specifically break the jar in front of these men and use that act to symbolically interpret the will of the Lord. This is the old covenant practice of prophecy that continues in the early church life and ministry. The Lord gives Peter a symbolic vision on three occasions in order to prepare his heart for what the Father wanted to do with the Gentiles (see Acts 10:10–20). Agabus, a prophet, used Paul's own belt to bring him a prophetic word about his future (see Acts 21:10–11).

There are many, many references in scripture in all the prophetic books where God spoke creatively with prophets using signs, symbols, objects, and everyday occurrences to convey His will and His word. He moves easily in partnership with the natural world and the supernatural realm.

I once spoke to a church that had become moribund in their faith and approach to God. The Lord told me to buy a particular plant that had become pot bound. That is, its roots had filled the pot to such an extent that they had no further room to expand.

HAVE FUN AND BE AMAZED!

If it remains in this pot, the plant will die for lack of nutrients and growing space.

I was instructed to set a table at the front of the meeting and to bring a larger pot, compost and potting soil, and lots of water. I brought two pot-bound plants. Carefully removing one plant from its prison, I showed the church the problem and the danger this plant was facing. Then I relayed to them the prophetic message of their own spiritual condition, comparing it with the plant. Finally, I took a hammer and broke the second pot, freeing the plant from its confines, and repotted it in a large pot, prophesying all the time regarding what the Lord wanted to do with each individual life. Finally, as I watered the plant the Lord gave a beautiful promise concerning the influx of the Holy Spirit to create new life and momentum. What followed was several hours of personal ministry as people repented and responded. When I first displayed the pot-bound plants, they were sick looking and unhealthy. By the end of the evening one plant was dead and the repotted one was bursting with health. The Father loves such imagery. He created us to be seers as well as listeners.

Many, many times I have seen the Lord intervene in people's lives in this manner, bringing release and new freedom to know Him and explore His will.

When we approach prophecy through the very heart of God, we find an anointing to speak that communicates on several levels. We learn not to be one dimensional in our approach to conveying the word of the Lord. He is wonderfully creative, and to represent Him well we need to be touched and established by His ingenious, imaginative, and stimulating originality.

The Holy Spirit is amazing! Therefore it is our role to be amazed by the Father and to be gently nudged in the direction of the marvelous way that He communicates Himself.

Study this book and do the exercises and assignments in whatever order the Holy Spirit determines. Please, please, enjoy the process of learning, discovering, and becoming more. You will be astonished at what the Holy Spirit will show you and also at His wonderful demeanor. He is so ready to help you. Have fun and be at peace.

THE PROCESS *of* PROPHECY

REFLECTIONS

The following exercises are designed with this particular chapter in mind. Please work through them carefully before going on to the next chapter. Take time to reflect on your life journey as well as your prophetic development. Learn to work well with the Holy Spirit and people whom God has put around you so that you will grow in grace, humility, and wisdom in the ways of God.

Graham

REFLECTIONS, EXERCISES, AND ASSIGNMENTS

WHAT CONSTITUTES MATURITY?

How we undertake a task tells an awful lot about us. Our identity, mindset, experience, and creativity are all evidenced in the life that we bring to each assignment—so too are our attitude, our demeanor, and our standing in God. Our identity comes to the surface when we engage in any enterprise. Our doing reveals the current state of our being.

Prophecy is a commitment of the heart to speak in a way that edifies, encourages, and releases comfort. It is never casual nor matter-of-fact. Prophecy is spiritual, not logical. It is an affair of the heart and issues forth from a life that is fully engaged in experiencing the Lord. Prophecy that comes from God's heart will reengage another's heart before God, which will unlock their mind to be changed and renewed.

Heart prophecy is intuitive, creative, and powerful. It raises everyone's sights so that they can see God more clearly and see themselves in Him. When people prophesy, we see who they are in Christ. Within the context of this chapter, you must be willing and able to demonstrate these attributes as a sign of your growing maturity.

God loves us with all His heart and mind. It is vital that your mind is renewed in Christ and that your words carry the evidence of deep thought. Allow the Spirit to think in a powerful way in your own life situations. Know how the spirit of revelation works in life and ministry. The heart sees and our mind connects with that revelation to create prophecy that is crafted and effective. Your prime place of engagement is with the heart of God, then the mind of God. Are your logic and reason preventing you from being and doing what the Father is seeing and saying? Heart prophecy is inspirational and transforming. We need the heart of the Father, the mind of Christ, and the impetus of the Holy Spirit in each prophecy we bring.

God is surrounded by joy. He abides in incredible happiness. Heaven is full of laughter, singing, and joyous living. Our joy in life is meant to be full. Enjoy the prophetic and enjoy God's presence. Do you have pleasure in stillness and being quiet? Do you make time simply to listen?

Your confidence level in the goodness of God for you must operate at a high level to be consistent and continuous in the prophetic gift. We cannot visit confidence occasionally, we must live there habitually. What you are in God, you transmit in prophecy. Authentic prophecy flows from a genuine experience that is current. Who are you in Christ?

To pursue love is to run hard after God's heart. It is to get in His face every day. Love grows by pursuit. What are you seeking for right now regarding the heart of God in your own life? Sensitivity to the Holy Spirit arises out of a heart that has been touched and is easily aligned with the Father. Everyone who connects with you should be touched by the Lord; is this true of you? What amazes, astonishes, and astounds you about God? What does your present fullness consist of that gives testimony to who God is for you? Your current life and experience of God drive your prophetic expression.

Life in the Spirit is built on knowing who Jesus is for you. Within that revelation of Him, identity is formed and attachment commences, which leads us into a partnership that transcends mere ministry. Prophecy is not what we do; it is who we are. We become encouragement. We are comforters. We are builders who love to make God bigger. We adore growth and we are as jealous as God to see people do well in Him. In partnership we become subconcious stewards of His goodness and kindness, and other people see it in us and respond to the Lord. When people are around you, are they expectant of God? Do they connect with who He is for them? Do they catch the spirit of His love, joy, and peace?

If your heart is fully attuned to the Father, then you are a reconciliation ministry with power to restore. The world beats people up, the kingdom of heaven renews, refreshes, and revives them. The Father is wonderfully creative in His ability to make all things new. Scripture is a visual revelation of the promises of God being fulfilled. Prophecy and Scripture have an excellent partnership that allows us massive freedom to be artistic, imaginative, clever, ingenious, inspired, inventive, and original.

If your heart and mind are renewed in Christ, then you have access to the Creator within. God has never stopped being creative. Ask the Lord to engage with you creatively in prophecy. When your mind is renewed, your imagination can serve the Lord.

WHAT CONSTITUTES IMMATURITY?

It is not what goes into a man's mouth that defiles him, it is what comes out. To prophesy the heart of God, there must be a purity in our normal conversation and language. A fountain cannot issue forth sweet water and bitter. Your mouth is the expression of what is in your heart.

Are you holding grudges, resentment, unforgiveness? Do you enjoy sarcasm? Are you good at making fun of others? Of course there is a lighthearted banter that exists between good friends. This is more than that and may lead to cynicism, mocking, and derisive communication.

Prophecy is never casual but intentional. It has depth. Immature prophecy is crude, unprepared, unformed, and childish. There is a difference between immature prophecy and inexperience. The latter is new, green, unpracticed, and comes from a life that is learning how to be familiar with the beauty of the Lord. It is unskilled in the art of using words to inspire and strengthen others, but it loves the training.

Immature people never work hard at relationships. They do not listen and do not retain what they learn because they never practice it until it becomes intuitive and therefore established in their life. Immature people are usually pessimistic. They seldom take ground and hold it; so eventual defeat follows any gain they may make because they do not persevere.

Prophecy must be pure. There can be no mixture in motive. We cannot influence others for our own gain. We cannot use prophecy to make a point. Prophecy is not magic. It has to be followed up with obedience and surrender in the recipient. There is no breakthrough without follow-through. Immature prophecy guarantees an outcome outside of obedience and renouncing of sin and error. Prophecy works with the cross of Christ and indeed points to it.

When people are in sin, we need to see them through God's eyes in Christ. The prophetic word must lead them to a joyful capitulation to the mercy, forgiveness, and purity of the Lord.

Our lack of relationship with God will be seen and noted over a period of time. Immaturity is holding to a place of being double-minded so that we flip-flop from a right way to a wrong way of thinking, seeing, living, and being. We cannot entertain doubts and trust God. These two cannot coexist in the same space at the same time. One of them has to go and we get to choose. Likewise, we cannot have anxiety and peace living together, nor fear and love; callousness and compassion; meanness and kindness; exasperation and forbearance; irritation and patience, to name just a few anomalies that can afflict us. Immaturity is either not choosing or choosing poorly. Mostly it is our lack of pleasure in who God is for us that encourages such negativity. What are you displaying of the fruit of the Spirit? Anxiety speaks louder than words.

When our soul is not under the rule of our spirit, it is impossible to become continuously confident. Our soul, when in charge, always seeks reassurance. We believe the worst, not the best. In days of difficulty we do not express the luxury of hope. Hope is expectation of the goodness of God coming through on our behalf. Hope understands future grace and knows that everything is more than covered by the goodness of God. I am free to make an honest mistake and the Father's love will cover it. An undeveloped life cannot carry the anointing over time and distance. If you want the anointing to be heavy, then your heart must be light and your rest must be big (see Matthew 11:28–30). Rest is a weapon. Weariness is a liability. Is your soul or your spirit prominent in your life? The fruit of the Spirit is the prime indicator of spirituality. What are you modeling consistently?

Some people have minds like a vacuum cleaner: they suck up any old rubbish. Immaturity is present when we fail to love God with our mind. Our thought life should aid our heart in worship, not hinder it. When logic and reason mean more to us than wisdom and revelation, our knowledge of God cannot lead us into fruitful experience. The mind of Christ is intuitive, not reasonable. The thinking of God is imaginative, not logical. Prophecy reflects the way God is in His creative self. Walking around Jericho for a week saying nothing is illogical; so too is shouting and expecting fortified walls to fall down! That was the prophetic instruction.

We are immature when our knowledge of God has not led us into an experience of who He is in the realm that we are discovering. When scripture reveals one thing and our lifestyle another, immaturity is the evidence.

Indifference to people's life condition is a form of adolescent immaturity. Whilst it is true that we each have giftings and callings that are inclined toward certain people groups, there will always be the times when we are moved with compassion for someone who may be outside our normal remit.

To have no compassion is immature. It often can signal a preoccupation with self. Learning to see people through the eyes of God makes us present to the moment in a crowd of strangers! Seeing negatively is a sign of immaturity. So too is speaking out continuously what you have not appropriated by experience.

Do you know your own identity in Christ? Are you aware of your own inheritance? Immature people speak out as ones who are not fully engaged in their own journey of discovery. We may not be aware of the fullness of our destiny, but we must be on the road to discovery and having experiences.

NOTES

NOTES

NOTES

NOTES

AN ASSIGNMENT

Think of a person in your life at this time who seems to be prone to anxiety and worry.

READ LUKE 10:38-42

This is a human allegory about spirit and soul. It is about the paradox of being and doing. A paradox is two apparently opposing ideas contained in the same truth. In a paradox the issue is about both/and, not either/or. When a paradox is under stress, the issue is one of primacy, which is most important.

In this case primacy is dictated by "one thing is needful." It is concerned with the discipline of beholding and becoming like Jesus. It is about the priority of right relationship.

1. What is the one thing your friend must do at this time?

2. What specific encouragement can you give that would inspire your friend to forsake anxiety for trust?

3. How would you give the word in a way that would enable them to resolve to change?

4. What particular promise do you sense that the Lord is wanting to release into this person's life at this time?

5. Write the word on a card and mail it. Alternatively, write the word down for them but also speak it to them.

NOTES

NOTES

IMAGE OF GOD

We are all made in the image of God. How we perceive ourselves in Christ will seriously enable us to empower others in the Spirit.

1. What must change in your own self-image?

2. What are the things you most dislike about yourself?

3. What are the scriptures/promises that mean the most to you regarding your identity?

4. What is the next thing that God wants to develop regarding your image?

5. You may have a list of things to change about yourself! Pick the top one and concentrate on that only. Don't be worried over the others. We move ahead one breakthrough at a time.

6. What is the antidote to that particular poor image?

7. For example, if an inclination to worry is defining your image into being an anxious, fearful person, then the antidote is confidence. Look up confidence in scripture and study it for the next few weeks.

8. If you were to prophesy over an anxious person, you would have an objective to release them into confidence. What would you write to them?

9. Write to yourself, read it, and apply it.

NOTES

NOTES

CASE STUDY: MATCHING PROPHETIC DELIVERY WITH CONTENT

The delivery of a prophetic word must match its content. One cannot grab someone by the throat and prophesy love and peace; likewise, a prophecy about warrior strength cannot be properly prophesied in an airy whisper. The context must match the content.

Below are a few prophetic words I have given to individuals enrolled in my prophetic schools (I have changed the names for privacy reasons). In this exercise, read the prophetic word and answer the questions following it.

PROPHETIC WORD

Brian, I sense that the Lord is about to come and reveal Himself to you as a warrior and as your King. There have been seasons where He has come to you as a lover and a Father but now He is going to come as a King, as Captain of the Lord of Hosts. He is coming to you like this because this next season of your life is about you becoming more warlike. There is a warfare spirit that is going to come upon your life, your worship, your thanksgiving, and your praise. You're going to come to a whole new level of understanding the sovereignty, supremacy, and majesty of Jesus.

Every situation that comes into your life in the next season is to teach you about the sovereignty of God. He has a strength and power that He is going to pour into your life in these next days. It will cause you to rise up on the inside in warfare. There is a spirit of breakthrough in this next season in your life where you'll learn about the power and capacity that's in you to break through for yourself. The Lord says all of your own situations are fair game; every situation that you're coming into is about you triumphing. It's about you breaking through and about you breaking out.

When you pray, when you intercede, God will take you to a place of proclamation and declaration. You will declare to the enemy that he can go this far but no further. There is an anointing upon you to come into the lives of others and say, "I'm drawing a line here and you're not coming across that line, because the Spirit of God forbids you. This is where it stops." There is an anointing upon you to cause breakthrough in the hearts and lives of other people. Your whole prophetic spirit is about releasing captives—you will go against the oppressor, grab his hand, and unclench his fist so that he lets go of people. You will pull his hand away from people and declare freedom into people's lives. The Lord says that He has put a sword in your hand and everywhere you go you're going to hear the sound of chains hitting the floor.

ANSWER THE FOLLOWING QUESTIONS

1. What is the crux (focus) of this word?

2. What are the emotion and plan God has for Brian?

3. What would be the best way to deliver this word? What tone of voice would be best to use? What body language and position should be used?

4. After delivering the word, what would you pray over him?

If the objective of a prophecy is to give strength and power, then you're not going to say it like this: *Um, I just uh, uh really sense that uh, the uh, um, the Lord really wants to um, uh, that He, uh, He really um, that the Lord wants to uh, come and uh He really wants you to um, be strong.* This isn't going to breed confidence: it just leads the listeners to think, *God, help him. Save him; do something; take him to glory; get him out of our sight. Who is this poor child?* The objective is lost.

NOTES

NOTES

NOTES

NOTES

NOTES

NOTES

NOTES

LECTIO DIVINA

Lectio Divina (Latin for *divine reading*) is an ancient way of reading the Bible—allowing a quiet and contemplative way of coming to God's Word. *Lectio Divina* opens the pulse of the Scripture, helping readers dig far deeper into the Word than normally happens in a quick glance-over.

In this exercise, we will look at a portion of Scripture and use a modified *Lectio Divina* technique to engage it. This technique can be used on any piece of scripture; I highly recommend using it for key Bible passages that the Lord has highlighted for you, and for anything you think might be an inheritance word for your life (see the *Crafted Prayer interactive journal* for more on inheritance words).

READ THE SCRIPTURE (1 CORINTHIANS 14:1-5, 26-33, 39-40)

Pursue love, and desire spiritual gifts, but especially that you may prophesy. For he who speaks in a tongue does not speak to men but to God, for no one understands him; however, in the spirit he speaks mysteries. But he who prophesies speaks edification and exhortation and comfort to men. He who speaks in a tongue edifies himself, but he who prophesies edifies the church. I wish you all spoke with tongues, but even more that you prophesied; for he who prophesies is greater than he who speaks with tongues, unless indeed he interprets, that the church may receive edification.

How is it then, brethren? Whenever you come together, each of you has a psalm, has a teaching, has a tongue, has a revelation, has an interpretation. Let all things be done for edification. If anyone speaks in a tongue, let there be two or at the most three, each in turn, and let one interpret. But if there is no interpreter, let him keep silent in church, and let him speak to himself and to God. Let two or three prophets speak, and let the others judge. But if anything is revealed to another who sits by, let the first keep silent. For you can all prophesy one by one, that all may learn and all may be encouraged. And the spirits of the prophets are subject to the prophets. For God is not the author of confusion but of peace, as in all the churches of the saints.

Therefore, brethren, desire earnestly to prophesy, and do not forbid to speak with tongues. Let all things be done decently and in order.

1. Find a place of stillness before God. Embrace His peace. Chase the nattering thoughts out of your mind. Calm your body. Breathe slowly. Inhale. Exhale. Inhale. Exhale. Clear yourself of the distractions of life. Whisper the word "stillness." Take your time. When you find that rest in the Lord, enjoy it. Worship Him in it. Be with Him there.

2. Read the passage twice. Allow its words to become familiar to you. Investigate Paul's encouragement to prophesy. What images does

it bring to your spirit? What do you see? Become a part of it. What phrases or words especially resonate with you? Meditate especially on those shreds of revelation. Write those pieces down in your journal.

3. Read the passage twice again. Like waves crashing onto a shore, let the words of Scripture crash onto your spirit. What excites you? What scares you? What exhilarates you about this revelation of the love of God? What are you discerning? What are you feeling? What are you hearing? Again, write it all down in your journal.

4. Write the theme of this passage in your journal.

5. Does this passage rekindle any memories or experiences? Does it remind you of any prophetic words you have given or received? Write those down as well.

6. What is the Holy Spirit saying to you through this scripture? Investigate it with Him — picture the two of you walking through it together. Write those words in your journal.

7. Read the passage two final times. Meditate on it. Is there something God wants you to do? Is there something He is calling you to? Write it down.

8. Pray silently. Tell God what this passage is saying to you. Tell Him what you are thinking about. Write down your conversation together. Picture yourself and the Holy Spirit as two old friends in a coffee shop, chatting about what God is doing.

9. Finally, pray and thank God for His relationship with you. Come back to the passage once a week for the next three months. Read it and let more revelation flow into you. If you feel compelled to, craft a prayer based on this passage for yourself, your family, your friends, or your church. Pray that prayer until you feel God has birthed it in you.

NOTES

NOTES

NOTES

NOTES

NOTES

NOTES

NOTES

NOTES

A MEDITATION AND EXPLANATION EXERCISE

To meditate means to think deeply about something or someone. It means to explore with mind and heart, allowing what you think to touch your innermost being.

Meditation is creative thought that leads us to the higher realm of revelation and wisdom. It takes us beyond the place of reason to where joy is seated and faith is activated.

Meditation allows us to search inside and outside the box of our current paradigm. What you see and hear there touches you profoundly. It adds a ring around the core truth of Christ that is God within, the certainty of freedom.

Fruitful meditation is therefore not a casual seeking for revelatory insight. Initial creative thoughts are merely the X that marks the spot. There is treasure in meditation, a guarantee of wealth in the pursuit of God.

Many are satisfied with collecting random truth on the surface of their consciousness. It is good wholesome stuff but it does not satisfy and it cannot challenge the complexities of life in a warfare context.

Deep truth has to be mined over days and weeks. It takes joy and patience to take truth down to its deepest level—beyond meeting our current needs, beyond the depth of understanding the power it releases to us against our adversary—down to the depth where God lives in the highest places of heaven. For all meditation must ultimately come before the throne of His majesty, sovereignty, and supremacy. He fills all things with Himself.

Our current situation requires wisdom, but even more it yearns for presence. Meditation allows us to experience both, through the word coming alive in our spirit. Meditation leads us to God and the permission of His heart. Learn to be in the question peacefully with God. Let the Holy Spirit teach you how to abide. Turn inwardly and rest; wait patiently. He will come. When your heart gets restless, turn to worship. When the interior atmosphere settles, return to listening.

Write down initial thoughts but do not pursue them just yet. Do not be distracted by what you hear initially. Set it aside; come back to it later.

When first entering a lifestyle of meditation, take care to ease into it slowly—an hour at first, then longer until half a day, and so on.

Always have a focus; do not try to wait in a vacuum. In this next exercise is a particular statement, followed by a series of questions. This is both to give you practice in meditation and to bring you into revelation of God through the focus statement. Use the questions as the Spirit leads. This exercise is not prescriptive but merely a guide to enable your contemplation. No doubt you will discover better questions as the Holy Spirit tutors you. Enjoy!

MEDITATION EXERCISE

"...stand in your problem, holding onto the promise, looking for the provision."

Engage your heart with the picture this statement provokes.

What does this mean for you?

What problems currently require God's blessing?

What particular promise is the Holy Spirit drawing to your attention? Ask for scriptural support.

Study the promise(s). Look for key words and phrases. Write down specifically what the Lord is guaranteeing to you in your current circumstances.

How will you stand and position yourself before the Father?

What level of confidence does the Father wish to bestow upon you?

What fear, unbelief, and inadequacy must you give up in favor of the promise?

View the promise and the provision together until they fill your vision and hope/faith begin to rise.

Now, through the lens of the promise, look at the problem. What has changed in your: heart? viewpoint? mindset?

Compose a prayer before the Lord, a request for His grace, kindness and power to enable you to receive.

Write a psalm of thanksgiving to the Lord for what He has done in and for you in this current situation.

Write out in full a confession and a declaration that you can speak into your circumstances by the power of the Holy Spirit.

As you challenge your circumstances with your newfound revelation, a boldness and confidence will enter your speech. How did you feel?

Continue declaring, believing, and challenging daily until God speaks further or the problem disappears.

What has changed in you?

What have you learned?

What have you become in Christ?

Finally, enter all these things in your journal. Keep a record of your walk with God in this way not only to encourage you in later times but also as a legacy to your family and friends.

WHAT KIND OF PARTNERSHIP WITH LEADERS?

1. Leaders are looking for appropriate levels of accountability and a developing sense of responsibility.

2. Leaders love a teachable spirit when loving feedback is given regarding methodology and presentation of prophecy.

3. Leaders want the personal life and relationships of people moving in gifting to have appropriate levels of Christlike behavior.

4. Leaders are looking for a servant spirit in which to invest and develop a greater sense of responsibility for the body as a whole.

5. A partnership should begin with prophecies that release encouraging, edifying, and comforting words and only then progresses as capability increases.

6. Develop meetings where prophecy can be targeted at specific people, problems, and situations. Follow up with prayer.

7. Give personal input to develop a greater perception of God.

8. Where necessary provide specific opportunity to upgrade personality to a more positive outlook.

9. Be generous but tough when people are not getting the message.

10. Provide a team context in which to learn and develop gifting. Provide a team leader who is part of the wider leadership team.

WHAT HELP AND SUPPORT FROM LEADERS?

1. Prophetic people need encouragement and constructive feedback on their gifting, methodology, and content of their words.

2. Guidelines need to be issued that allow people the freedom to upgrade and improve their gifting.

3. People need to be free to make mistakes while learning humility, honesty, and accountability.

4. Develop workshops to provide opportunities for practice, practice, and more practice. Offer dialogues and discussions on case histories, right habits, and improved content and presentation.

5. There should be training in the church on the disciplines of hearing and waiting on God through meditation, listening prayer, and contemplation.

6. There should be devotional training that teaches people how to relate, respond, and be intimate in worship to God.

7. Upgrade the level of prophecy in the church through a deliberate partnership and loving relationship.

8. Provide practical loving support when people get it wrong, not just to close down their gift. People do not learn successfully in a vacuum. To restrain people without development is actually punishment.

9. Prophetic people need a place in which to use and develop their gifting, ideally a small group setting, in order to encourage their movement and minimize any mistakes.

10. Prophetic people need a focus that has been agreed upon with the leadership regarding their own development. It should be in the form of an action plan that at least agrees with the parameters for this next season.

NOTES

A PROPHECY: VICTORIES FROM A NEW LENS

THE LORD SAYS, DO NOT look at the next twelve months in the way you've looked at the last ten years. I'm giving you new eyes, I'm giving you a new heart, and I am giving you a new mind. You will perceive totally differently. You will believe more freely and you will think the way I think. Because this is what I am doing, I am elevating your thinking to My level. You will think on a level that I think. You will behold in the spirit what I am beholding. You will understand what I'm holding out to you and you will take the provision of your God and spread it around in your own life.

You will come into a place of successive, easy, and quick victories. There will be some situations when I will hold up victory for a while so that your revenge can be complete.

There will be times when I will allow the enemy to contend with you so that I may establish you in something deep and powerful and profound. When you come into a situation that is resisting you, I want you to smile. Because the hand of your God, I intend through the resistance to give you a double portion. It is not about what the enemy is doing. It is about what I am allowing. I will allow him to come against you so that I may give you a double portion and that I may increase the anointing upon you in those days.

Your life will be a balance of easy victories and times when the enemy will contend, but it is on those days of contention that I have a divine increase for you. Look for increase in a time when the power seems to have slowed down. Look for the increase and stand and worship.

You will know Me, for I will reveal Myself to you and I will come to you. I will establish in you the very things that I want you to have and you will behold the power of your God. You will start to think with a level of wisdom and intelligence you have never seen before; you will start to see in the realm of the spirit in a way you've never seen before.

Out of your mouth will come words of faith. You will completely lose the ability to worry or be anxious because I am making war on anxiety. I am making war on panic. I am making war on fear. You will not be subject to those things but will know your God. You will be strong in your God and you will do exploits this next twelve months. You will do exploits in your own life.

When those things are established in you, I will lead you. I will bring you across the path of people who are victims in the area you have just won through. You will assist them, you will help them, and you will be a breakthrough anointing to them. As they break through, your anointing will go to a deeper level still; and as you give out so the anointing in you will increase and abide and will abound. In this way, in the next twelve months you will make years and years of growth.

You will become the man and woman you were always supposed to be and you will come into a place where nothing will overwhelm you. You will come into a place where you will cease to be a foot soldier in the body of Christ. You will take on the stature of a warrior. You will take on the stature of David's mighty men. I will cause a greatness to rise up within you. I will make you a power in the land.

Even as you come to the end of this twelve months of training, I will begin to show you and declare to you what your personal inheritance is so that you may be a stakeholder in the territory of the spirit that I choose to bestow upon you. You will come into your ministry. You will come into your anointing. You will come into a place of abundance. You will certainly and most definitely and assuredly come into the place of your favor. You will know that the hand of God is upon you. You will know what your assignment is, you will know who you are, you will know your identity, and you will know your inheritance. You will begin to stand in and trade upon the favor that is present over your life.

Then, when that quickening spirit has done that work, I will open a window in heaven and I'll pour things out upon you because this next twelve months is just the beginning. It's just boot camp. It's to get you up to speed with who I am, and then the real adventure begins.

RECOMMENDED READING

Title	Author	Publisher
Hearing God	Dallas Willard	InterVarsity Press
The Gift of Prophecy	Jack Deere	Vine Books
Surprised by the Voice of God	Jack Deere	Zondervan
Growing in the Prophetic	Mike Bickle	Kingsway
The Seer	James Goll	Destiny Image
Prophetic Etiquette	Michael Sullivant	Creation House
The Prophets' Notebook	Barry Kissel	Kingsway
User Friendly Prophecy	Larry Randolph	Destiny Image
Prophecy in Practice	Jim Paul	Monarch Books
Can You Hear Me?: Tuning in to the God Who Speaks	Brad Jersak	Trafford Press
When Heaven Invades Earth	Bill Johnson	Treasure House
Knowledge of the Holy	A. W. Tozer	O. M. Publishing
The Pleasures of Loving God	Mike Bickle	Creation House
Manifest Presence	Jack Hayford	Chosen
Living the Spirit-Formed Life	Jack Hayford	Regal
The Agape Road	Bob Mumford	Lifechangers
The Sensitivity of the Spirit	R. T. Kendall	Hodder & Stoughton
Living in the Freedom of the Spirit	Tom Marshall	Sovereign World

Title	Author	Publisher
Secrets of the Secret Place	Bob Sorge	Oasis House
The Heart of Worship	Matt Redman	Regal
Experiencing the Depths of Jesus Christ	Jeanne Guyon	Seedsowers
The Unsurrendered Soul	Liberty Savard	Bridge-Logos

ABOUT THE PROPHETIC EQUIPPING SERIES

Graham began teaching prophetic schools in 1986. Eight years later he wrote *Developing Your Prophetic Gifting*, a book that has won universal acclaim. Translated into numerous languages, reprinted many times over, and published by several companies, it has been a best seller and is widely regarded as a classic. Graham has continued to develop new material each year in the Schools of Prophecy. Now after almost twenty years of teaching and continuously upgrading material, the School of Prophecy has developed into one of the finest teaching programs on the prophetic gift, ministry, and office of a prophet. This new material effectively makes *Developing Your Prophetic Gifting* redundant.

The Prophetic Equipping Series is an ongoing writing project that combines classic teaching with the journal format so popular in the *Being with God Series*. It also embraces training assignments, workshops, and reflective exercises, with emphasis on producing one of the finest teaching aids on the prophetic gift and ministry. These manuals are appropriate for individual, small-group, or church-wide use. All Christians can prophesy and would benefit from Graham's wisdom and experience in ministry. The assignments, exercises, workshops, *lectio divina* and other material are designed to further the understanding of the prophetic gift, ministry, and office. If used properly, the process will develop accountability for prophetic people, promote healthy pastoring of the prophetic, and give relevant questions for leadership and prophetic people to ask one another.

ABOUT THE AUTHOR

Graham Cooke and his wife, Theresa, live in Santa Barbara where they quide and interact with several communities that are millennial, entrepreneurial, and focused on the city.

Graham has a leadership and consulting role in a variety of groups and organizations at regional, national, and international levels. He is a mentor to ministries and works in various think tanks to promote Kingdom initiatives.

Theresa has a passion for worship and dance. She loves intercession cares about injustice and abuse, and has compassion for those who are sick, suffering, and disenfranchised.

Together they have two sons, three daughters, and eight grandchildren! They also have two other daughters in Australia who are part of their extended family.

Graham is involved in three aspects of ministry, each of which has a business model attached. These are:

BrilliantPerspectives.com—the consulting and training group that produces a range of messages across the spectrum of life in Christ, church development, and Kingdom engagement.

BrilliantBookHouse.com—the online resource for the physical and digital production of all Graham's messages, conferences, and school series, plus all his books and prophetic soaking words that have had a profound impact on individuals, families, and churches around the world.

BrilliantTV.com—our online streaming platform with thousands of subscribers receiving constant, consistent discipleship training and personal development input through a curated online community that is worldwide.